Every Time We Say Goodbye

For Charlotte

we didn't really need any anyway.

'Is he hmmmmmmmmmmmm, hmmmmmm or hmm?' I would ask when Dad went to interview anyone Israeli.

In the evenings Dad's girlfriend, Shirley, liked to go jogging and we would follow her up hills in the beige Volvo, watching her yellow satin shorts flap up and down in front of the crawling car. I stood on top of the Mount of Olives and sang *The Sound of Music* to the fuzzy pastelled sunset.

One day we went out to the West Bank to visit Dad's fixer and I was forbidden from eating anything in case I caught amoebas. Mohammed's mum, whose head-dress had tinkling coins round the front, was serving delicious-looking delicacies ('Don't be stupid. It's some old goat's eye'). She fetched them from her stove above where the animals were kept and Dad, I noticed, was stuffing them down and cheerfully swilling mint tea. We sat outdoors (in fact the house didn't have an indoors to speak of) and I went into the grove at the back with the fixer to pick grapes and olives from the grey trees. It was very hot. I developed a crush on this fixer who wore maroon loafers and white socks and had reflector shades. He was probably about twenty.

A huge crowd of ragged, grinning children ran in from the village to look at my hair, which was long and blonde. I let them all touch it one by one and they giggled and let me hold a little yellow chick they had brought with them.

But most days at the American Colony were spent by the pool with the tabloid hacks while Dad went out investigating. My companions would listen to the BBC World Service and rush upstairs to file copy when anything salient was announced. The lifeguard, Mohammed, taught me the Arabic I'm still using today. 'Hello. Hi. Thank you. Thank you very much. How are you? Fine. So so. Shit. Enough.' It never fails me. After I had left he wrote me a letter telling me he loved me.

I read my book, got a serious tan for the first time and swam a lot.

Diary, Monday 16 August 1982: Got up at 7.30 and went for a cold swim with a gay bloke here called Graham. He's nice. Got Dad and Shirley up and ate breakfast. Dad sat there for hours reading the papers and talking to the other journalists. I was bored. Then we all went to lots of travel agents all of whom were Israeli and said 'Shalom'. Dad tied Shirley's laces together.

This was the day before the night we went to Lebanon. We had to leave at 4a.m., so I retired to bed at six in the evening to ensure a good night's sleep. The others decided to stay up. 'Lovely day!' I chirped into the darkness at a specially laid on breakfast. Nobody answered me. Nobody looked well. We piled into two cars, one of which Dad was driving. I had to sit in the back although everyone knew I got carsick. I sulked. I can still see and feel the black plastic mats on the car floor and smell the cigarette smoke generated by five hungover, chain-smoking foreign correspondents. I wore my straw hat.

Diary, Tuesday, 17 August 1982: Was called at 3.30 and got ready and did final packing. Hotel dark. Got Dad and Shirley up and we (and Phil, Bill, Ancient Hugh and Mrs Ancient) ate a prepared cold

EVERY TIME WE SAY GOODBYE

The Story of a Father and a Daughter

Anna Blundy

Century · London

This edition published by Century Books Limited 1998

1 3 5 7 9 10 8 6 4 2

Century
Random House UK Ltd, 20 Vauxhall Bridge Road, London SW1V 2SA

Arrow Books Ltd
Random House UK Ltd, 20 Vauxhall Bridge Road, London SW1V 2SA

Random House Australia (Pty) Limited
20 Alfred Street, Milsons Point, Sydney,
New South Wales 2061, Australia

Random House New Zealand Limited
18 Poland Road, Glenfield, Auckland 10, New Zealand

Random House South Africa (Pty) Limited
Endulini, 5a Jubilee Road, Parktown 2193, South Africa

Random House UK Limited Reg No 954009

A CIP catalogue record for this book
is available from the British Library

Papers used by Random House Limited are natural, recyclable products made
from wood grown in sustainable forests. The manufacturing processes conform to
the environmental regulations of the country of origin.

ISBN 0 7126 7802 6

Printed and bound in the United Kingdom by Mackays of Chatham plc,
Chatham, Kent

Acknowledgements

I would like to thank British Airways and American Airlines for so kindly upgrading me; Eros Hoagland, Tom Long, Michael Campbell Johnson and Gene Palumbo for all their help in El Salvador; Sister Pamela Hussey for reassuring me about the whole escapade; Deborah Rogers and Louise Hartley Davies for their encouragement throughout; Horatio Mortimer for bringing me sea breezes while I was writing and Sophia Schutts and Mark Mortimer for putting up with my snarling presence during the book's final stages.

David Blundy, a British journalist, died in El Salvador yesterday after being shot during fighting in the capital between Government troops and Left-wing rebels. Mr Blundy, 44, was struck by a single shot.

The Daily Telegraph, Saturday, 18 November, 1989.

Chapter One

Let Love clasp Grief lest both be drown'd,
Let darkness keep her raven gloss:
Ah, sweeter to be drunk with loss,
To dance with death, to beat the ground,

Than that the victor Hours should scorn
The long result of love, and boast:
'Behold the man that loved and lost,
But all he was is overworn.'

from *In Memoriam* by Alfred, Lord Tennyson

1989

There was a particular second when the world collapsed. I was sitting cross-legged on the floor of my rooms at Oxford on 17 November painting the backs of some ear-rings with anti-allergy ointment. It was about four o'clock in the afternoon and the little stone lions on the roof of All Souls were still just about visible, diligently clutching their spears in the twilight. I had picked up a fake emerald the size of a broad bean that I had bought that day to wear at a college dinner with the velvet dress my mother had lent me. The phone rang.

Ben Macintyre ('May his last strand of hair fall out,' Dad would have said) then worked at the same paper as my father, a new publication called the *Sunday*

1

Correspondent which has since folded, and I had met him the summer before in Washington, DC. We stood on Dad's balcony on P Street near Dupont Circle, smoked a packet of Winstons and watched the gay couples cavorting in front of Mr P's bar. I clenched the phone between cheek and shoulder and smiled at the receiver. I could feel the carpet under my bare feet and I curled my toes when Ben asked me if I was alone or not.

In a way I had been expecting this call all my life. When I was eleven and Dad was in Lebanon during the civil war he had told me what I would have to do if he got kidnapped. He gave me the numbers of his friends from the local television stations in Beirut and I was to call them, go over there, make televised appeals for his release and generally create as much public fuss as possible. I almost looked forward to it, imagining myself saving his life and being followed around by TV cameras in some sweltering minaretted city.

Once, Capital Radio reported that he had been arrested in Addis Ababa. In fact he was confined to his hotel room. The hotel in Addis put me through to his room and he answered. 'How are you?' I asked, confused. 'Fucking awful!' he said. 'You've given me fucking chickenpox and they've got me in quarantine.' I told him to pull himself together, and put the phone down laughing. We used to give each other quizzes over the phone. He would ask me who the Israeli foreign minister was and I would ask him who my form teacher was. We would both fail.

This time I knew Dad had gone to El Salvador. He hated Washington and would use any available excuse to got to Central America and see something interesting (people dying horribly). He couldn't stand the self-seriousness of the Washington scene – hanging out with besuited hacks who thought going to a presidential briefing made them presidential themselves.

Bored out of his mind, he wrote me letters with no capital letters, typed frantically on thin green printer-paper about the birds who had laid eggs on his balcony and about all the sad old hacks who would drink at his house.

'Dear Rat Features . . .' the letters would begin.

This one was sent from Washington, DC, dated 1989:

The birdies laid four little sky blue eggypops in the nest. In my new role as unemployed poofter I put bread out on the balcony and a bowl of water so they could have a nice bath before breakfast, a cup of coffee and a pile of rice crispies.

It remained untouched, so the next day I went out and got a bag full of 'wild bird seed'. This had a remarkable effect on the local wild life. The balcony was full of birds from morning to twilight, the noise of tweeting was so loud I couldn't sleep after 6am. But then, just as everything in the birdie kingdom looked fine, I peeped in the nest and two of the sodding eggs were gone, gone. I looked under the tree and not a single sign of egg shell. I called in the birdie homicide squad and yesterday I think I caught a glimpse of the homicidal maniac who did it. This big brown birdie about the size of a buzzard was hopping around eating mounds of wild bird seed and hopping up on the only living tree to look in the nest. I suspect it was trying to see whether there were any more little eggypops in it. Then it flapped off guiltily with the noise of a Boeing 747. I thought it had guilt written all over its beak so I've bought a bag of 'poisoned wild bird seed'. So that's it. No more eggs. No more birdies. And in a strange way it seems to be a symbol of my life at the moment.

Went out with the police but unfortunately no one was murdered or even shot. Someone was beaten half to death but I wasn't there – the photographer, Stuart, was luckily – because I was going to a poncy Georgetown party with my very close friends Senator Nunn, Senator Dodd, Senator Whatsit, Congressman Les Aspin and good old Lee Atwater the head of the National Republican Committee. It was such fun that me and Cockburn sloped off down to the rat and ferret at about 9-30pm.

This would go on for six pages and would end, typically, like this one.

I am probably going to Haiti on Saturday (March 4th) then onto Salvador or perhaps Honduras to see those nice contras. Phone me there, or don't bother as usual.

Love Daddikins

I had phoned him the day before it happened – eight years later I remember the number and I still flinch towards the phone when something makes me laugh. I heard the message with a hotel number in San Salvador on his answering machine – 'Hi, I'll be at the Camino Real on 503 . . .' I needed some money, I think, and I didn't bother to call the number. ('No, no, fine. Don't worry about your ageing father who's slaved away for you all his life. Milk me dry. I'll just survive on camel dung . . .')

'He's been shot in the chest. It looks pretty serious,' Ben said. That was it. The end of that life and the beginning of this new one.

People at college had heard the news on the radio – shot but still alive – and a few came up to see me. Ben's dad, Angus Macintyre who died in a car crash five years later, was a history don at Magdalen and he came breathless and kind to my rooms. 'He'll be all right,' he said. 'I feel it in my bones.' This expression has seemed sinister since – conjuring up splintered bones rather than certainty.

It was unimaginable I would never see him again. Dad had never been to Oxford but I could picture him slouching out of a hire car on the High Street, pulling his shabby khaki bag on to his shoulder, hunching his leather jacket up and looking for my college, peering through his glasses and being secretly impressed.

I have dreams in which he comes back and I say things like, 'I've got all your suitcases on top of my wardrobe' and 'You owe us £1,000 for that gravestone'. He laughs and explains how he was taken hostage or something.

While we waited for more news that night my boyfriend and I drank a bottle of port and smoked one cigarette after the other without noticing. Giles Coren is frozen in my mind the second before the end of everything, holding two carrier bags of shopping (a big plastic bottle of Cherryade in one), curls tumbling over his face. He emerged blinking from a studious alcove in the library as

I stood at one end and screamed for him. 'Dad's been shot!'

Eventually we took a taxi to Heathrow and the taxi driver refused to go over fifty miles an hour. It was cold and foggy. 'My father is dying in a hospital in El Salvador. A plane full of people is waiting for me. Go faster,' I spat. He ignored me. 'Funny that,' he said minutes later in the Oxford accent that I have hated since that moment. 'I had a rush job like this last night.'

The airport was bright and crowded, but immediately I saw Mum wearing a long coat and Ben, dishevelled, besuited and with £2,000 in an envelope in his pocket. Mum shook her head and turned down the edges of her mouth and I fainted for a second or two. I remember the fall and an airhostessy escort to a hospitality room. On the low table there was a little basket with brown plastic mini-cartons of milk in it. The people were allowed to take off for Miami. There was no need for us to be there with him (I had imagined him laughing about our fuss. Telling us to fuck off home and stop bothering him) – he wasn't anywhere any more.

On the way back to Crouch End in a black taxi we could hear the radio from the cab. *British journalist David Blundy was shot today in central San Salvador as the . . .* and then, *British journalist David Blundy was shot dead today as San Salvador's bloody civil war . . .* It was dark outside and rain was blurring the headlights on the motorway and the yellow glare of shops by the road. Mum kept talking about how nobody would pick up all his shirts from the dry cleaners. Ben kept saying 'Bastard!', as though Dad had always had a secret plan to go and get killed and leave us here in this empty boring world without him. He'd effected his plan without saying goodbye. Someone I never identified went all the way to Dulles airport in Washington, DC to put a bunch of flowers under the windscreen wipers of the car he would never collect.

At home Ricky, my stepfather, opened the front door in tears and I knelt on the grey carpet in front of a blue wicker table smoking Silk Cut Extra Mild and drinking a gin and tonic. It was the first time I had smoked in front of Mum and Ricky. The ITN news ran footage of Dad being rushed through a red dusty street into a hospital, covered in wires and drips, bare-chested. His eyes were open, cornflower blue and terrified. There was an oxygen mask over his mouth. They told me later he had lost consciousness in the van that took him to hospital, but it didn't look like it to me.

The phone kept ringing and I ate poached eggs on toast. The most terrible thing in the world happens and there you are doing something utterly banal – poaching an egg. I went upstairs to my room and read *Hotel du Lac*.

When I found I couldn't sleep I put on jeans and a sweatshirt and drove around London, way over the alcohol limit but still far more lucid than I wanted to be, in a Citroën Visa dad had bought me two years before on my seventeenth birthday. 'So that no ghastly spotty youths can drive you around and crash.' He had written 'Happy 17th Birthday – May It Be Your Last' on a piece of paper scrunched on to the aerial.

I found the piece of paper the other day, a hole in its middle.

I drove along the Embankment at 3.30a.m. screaming into the steering wheel and I remember watching the lights strung together like a necklace passing me by in a teary haze. I concentrated on wanting him to come back and on the image of him dead in the dust thousands of miles from home with nobody there who cared about him.

Someone said to me the other day, 'He doesn't sound like the kind of bloke who wanted anyone permanent, who had anyone at all.'

He had me, I thought. He had me.

Letter of condolence from my friend Andrew Meier,
November 1989
I've lost friends before – ones I've known better and longer, but none has made me think about the kind of life I want more than your Dad. Nothing of course could have been further from his mind. No one should try to make sense of death, let alone one so insane and tragic. But if there is any light in this darkness, it comes from knowing that he touched so many, who like me will join you in carrying his memory forever. And I'm pretty damn proud to be in your company.

Dad and I had always walked my dog, a border collie called Tess, in Waterlow Park and on Hampstead Heath. He had bought her for me on my thirteenth birthday. He had been desperate for Mum and me to get a dog for years, for reasons of security, he claimed. Mum wasn't having any of it. Every birthday and Christmas he would ask me what he should get me and I would say, 'A dog.' That year he said, 'Come on then,' and we drove to the dog shop.

Far from Tess's presence quelling his over-imaginative

fears for our safety in that notorious South Bronx of England, Crouch End, Dad became obsessed with the dog's safety and well-being, fearing her sudden death at every phone call. 'How's Tessy?' he'd ask, nervous. 'You mean . . . the Late Tessy . . .' I replied, cackling.

She is now, as of last September, the Late Tessy, finally consigning the whole period to a barely believable past.

When we walked her together Dad would insist on stopping in Waterlow Park at the fence that overlooks Highgate Cemetery from where you can see Karl Marx's tomb through a rambling avenue of crooked gravestones and dark ivy. 'It's the grimmest little park in the world,' he would say, delightedly peering up at the cemetery's smoking tower and across to the workhouse-like Victorian hospital where I was born. Having once seen a water rat by the park's gloomy pond he would stand staring at the water's edge for hours, encouraging the dog to hunt out the elusive creatures that Dad only liked for their vileness. I always wanted to hurry to Mr G's on Highgate Hill. It has now become Pizza Express. 'What? Mr G's gone! Gone?' They kept a bottle of Tabasco there for Dad although he was only in the country a couple of times a year. He would run next door to the deli and buy a tub of selected meats which he fed to Tess through the car window at five-minute intervals.

He sat chain-smoking, slurping espressos and rapping his fingers on the table while he complained about his life or interviewed my friends about theirs. 'I'm thinking of changing from physics,' my friend Lucy told him over a bowl of horrible spaghetti Bolognese. Dad was disappointed because he had always wanted Lucy to be an astronaut, but he was just about content to let her change if she did Arabic. 'I know lots of people you could stay with in Cairo,' he said, excited, and started rifling frantically through his address book giving this eighteen-year-old student the numbers of ministers, film stars and Nobel prize-winning authors. It didn't occur to him she might not call them. She did change to Arabic, though.

Letter of condolence from Lucy Clift, November 1989
I'm sorry for not having written sooner – my mother phoned me up the night before I was leaving for the Sinai desert. All I really wanted to tell you is just that I thought your dad was the coolest, funniest, and most fun to be with person I've ever known. I couldn't possibly forget the brilliant times I spent with you and him – even just taking Tess for a walk in Kenwood, and going for a coffee afterwards! I always really looked forward to the times when he'd be back home in London again. I still remember the time when I'd decided that my ambition was to be a flying doctor in Greenland/Australia (all the same really, aren't they?). Your dad was the only person I talked to about it who agreed that it was a brilliant idea. He was so special because he didn't just treat me like a little schoolfriend of his daughter's. Your dad taught me the first ever Arabic phrase I knew – ana sahafiya, I am a journalist.

I decided to bury him in our view of Marx. The earth was wet from the rain and on that December morning it was covered with sodden brown leaves. The grim church off Pond Square was packed and I sat at the front with Mum and my stepmother Samira Osman and sister Charlotte.

Lucy Clift's mother approached me. I hadn't seen her for five years at least and she looked tearful and forlorn. 'I'm here for Lucy,' she said.

Charlotte, who was just two, had a little dark blue coat on and neat shoes. The pine coffin was covered with white lilies. My boyfriend Giles and I had stopped at the florist's and I bought a bunch of freesias. I didn't know what to write so I scrawled 'Goodbye Daddy' with the fountain pen he had bought me eight months before and carried the flowers into the church where I held them on my lap. The vicar, knowing he was besieged by cynical, raddled old atheists, did his best with the sermon and said, 'But who knows, David might be up there now with the angels.'

Lots of people, including myself, laughed loudly. Religion had never seemed so empty and ridiculous. He's not up there with the fucking angels, I thought. He's lying right in front of you, mate – shot, autopsied, a mole on his right cheek, golden hair on his tanned arms, white marks on his chest where he'd got some lack of pigmentation condition from being in the sun too much, a wart on his left ankle and an appendix scar on his tummy. Look! My dad's in there, you sanctimonious idiot!

Hobgoblin nor foul fiend can daunt his spirit
He knows he at the end shall life inherit.

Mum, Sam and I went in the hearse to the cemetery but most people walked. Bob Geldof was there and a friend of mine, who said afterwards 'That was the worst day of my life', was convinced he had been staring at her. (He hadn't.) It was hard to get such a huge coffin up the muddy slope to the spot we had been allocated and I kept thinking the pall bearers might drop him. There was no space for everyone to stand near the grave, although the cemetery had positioned planks over the mud for access. There were so many old gravestones, trees, ivy and fallen monuments to the dead and people stood lurking behind them. I thought I might pass out when the vicar was doing all the 'ashes to ashes' business and throwing earth on to the box. When I went up to the edge to throw my flowers down I nearly fell in. I caught myself falling forwards and just about managed to change it into backwards instead so that Samira caught me. I led Charlotte to the grave and she dropped a rose down out of her tiny hand. Mum threw in a card which she had sent to Dad every Christmas since about 1823 and he would send it back again before the end of January. It had Snoopy on the front holding a wreath and it read 'Deck The Halls'. There was a brass plaque on the coffin – DAVID MICHAEL BLUNDY 1945–1989.

At the party everybody got very drunk. I could picture Dad there with all his friends, leaning on the mantelpiece smoking and talking to someone. I wanted to creep up under his arm and lean against him. 'Whaddyou want Rat Features?' he would say, drape his arm round me and carry on talking. I told this to the host, who said it was uncanny that I should have imagined it that way because Dad had been standing right exactly where I had pictured him only a couple of months earlier. That trip to London when I had waved him off from my mum's house and I was holding Tess's collar as she strained after him. He waved from the little red hire car as he turned the corner and I shut the door, sat back against it and cried. Perhaps a bit more than usual. I don't know. I never saw him again.

In the kitchen something surreal was going on. Three ex-girlfriends of my father who had done things like torment each other with late-night phone calls and throw suicidal jealousy fits were having a chat. 'You must be Shirley,' said one to another and they burst into tears and fell into each other's arms by the fridge. They laughed about his bathing habits and squealed, half laughing half crying, when they discovered he'd bought them the same presents. Hey, me too. A Waterman pen? Yup. A silver Ethiopian cross? Uh-huh.

I couldn't bear it. 'Dad! Come and look at this!' I wanted to scream. My uncle, whom Dad had always used as an example of ill humour although he was secretly fond of him ('Colonel Gaddafi has the wit and generosity of your Uncle Ivan'), was openly crying and so were countless grim-faced weather-beaten hacks who usually made Clint Eastwood seem fey and girlish.

The friend with the Geldof fantasy had been given a pair of pearl earrings by her own dying father a few years before. She removed one and rammed it through my ear where there hadn't been a hole. 'If it doesn't go septic, they'll watch over us,' she said. It didn't, but they didn't.

Chapter Two

He is not here; but far away
The noise of life begins again,
And ghastly through the drizzling rain
On the bald street breaks the blank day.

1997

My pre-departure hysteria lasted a good couple of weeks. It didn't occur to me for a moment that I might be able to go to El Salvador and come back alive. The precedents, after all, weren't great. I had been meaning to go since Dad was killed, but now that the tickets were booked I was a pathetic snivelling wreck. I harangued everyone I could think of who had ever been there and poked and prodded them about the dangers. Unfortunately most of them were eminent journalists who were largely oblivious to danger, immune to it.

'Is it? Oh. Well, yes, probably. Still, you'll have a fantastic time. There's this great little . . .'

Jon Snow, of Channel 4 news took me out for sushi round the corner from ITN at the top of Farringdon Road. He had been in Salvador with Dad but hadn't known him well. He was passionate about the country and had clearly had the time of his life during the war. Partly, he said, because it was a just cause and you really felt you were doing something worthwhile in exposing the atrocities and taking sides.

14

Everyone sane took sides in the war in El Salvador, which raged between 1980 and 1992. That is, one side. It was a clear-cut right/wrong thing. Briefly and very crassly, the oppressed and poverty-stricken peasants wanted some basic rights and began to fight for them – they became the Frente Faribundo Marti de Liberación Nacional (FMLN) rebels. The corrupt and hugely wealthy ruling classes heavily influenced the Salvadorean government and army, whose death squads murdered both guerrillas and thousands of innocent peasants and churchmen brutally and at random in an effort to crush the uprisings. The Reagan administration, fearing a repeat of Nicaragua and believing Communism to be on its very doorstep, drew a line in the sand and lavishly funded the Salvadorean government. Effectively, therefore, the US was quite directly financing the notorious government death squads who carried out the most appalling massacres country-wide. The western press took a predictable and utterly justifiable stance and was, naturally, loathed by the Salvadorean government for what was seen as a gross 'mis-interpretation' of events.

Over our bite-sized pieces of squid, salmon and yellowtail, Jon Snow and I talked about the escapism of being a foreign correspondent. I was in self-indulgent mode.

'I often wonder how he could do it?' I said. 'How he could leave a child in England and go off to the other side of the world. I'm sure I couldn't.'

Snow said he thought it was a compulsion, something you almost couldn't help doing. It didn't reflect in any way on Dad's feelings for me, he imagined, but it was a total abdication of responsibility and, in the case of

Salvador, it was a mission so perfectly clear that the excuses were watertight.

People were forever telling me how much Dad missed me when he was away, but missing someone is the easy part. Being there takes the effort.

Letter of condolence from Marianne Szegedy-Maszak,
November 1989
Dear Anna,

I mean neither to be presumptuous or intrusive by writing to you . . . I knew your father for only a very short time – the last two months of his life to be exact.

But one thing you must know. During a time of, shall we say, something less than euphoria for him, the thing that could cheer him up, in fact the subject that would always make him shine, was you. That he loved you was obvious, but his pride in you – your accomplishments, your wisdom, your humour – was the one part of his life that was an unconditional joy.

I had planned weeks of preparation for the trip, but all it really involved was going through the newspaper cuttings on El Salvador and on my father in the News International library at Wapping. I paced round and round the desks waiting for the man to bring the stuff I had asked for out of the vaults, and I looked away as he slapped them down on to the table in front of me. 'Here's El Salvador,' he said, producing six huge files. 'And that's your father.' Dad's file was small, with maybe thirty cuttings, yellowing and scraggy looking.

I started with the easy stuff. I read through things about

what Salvador is like today and wasn't especially encouraged. The first cutting I pulled out was this. *The Times*, Friday, 5 July 1996:

> JAIL PROTESTERS SEW UP MOUTHS. Eleven inmates involved in a 'lottery of death' and hunger strike in a prison in El Salvador have sewn up their mouths. The 11 are among 180 prisoners who are refusing to eat in protest at chronic overcrowding in the Santa Aña prison, 40 miles east of the capital. The inmates have threatened to kill four convicts who were chosen in a lottery last month. The four, who are due to die on July 12, have already been blessed by a priest.

I wasn't anticipating many laughs here. I read about the 'football war' between El Salvador and Honduras which began in June 1969, and about how El Salvador was the smallest Central American Republic (everything ever written about the country says 'El Salvador is about the size of Wales') and that its chief products are coffee, cotton, rice, maize, cacao, tobacco, indigo, sugar, lumber, balsam, gold and silver. In 1979 a Swiss envoy was shot dead. On 24 March 1980 in the chapel of the Hospital Divina Providencia, Archbishop Oscar Romero was murdered. Twenty people were killed at his funeral. And on 31 March 1980, a week after his thirty-fifth birthday, my father was there. He wrote that in front of him an old woman and a small child had disappeared under the mass of bodies.

I began to wonder as I leafed through the cuts detailing murder after murder why the government troops were killing unarmed peasants so liberally, and none of the pieces I read quite explained what the link was between the FMLN guerrillas and the peasants. With irritatingly brutal clarity, Dad explained it to me in a *Sunday Times* piece, 22 February 1981: 'Distinction between peasant and guerrilla is academic.' That was that. I read about twenty-seven people being beheaded in a government massacre in 1981. I tried to block out the conversations of the library staff that were going on right beside me and my stomach churned in terror as the hours went by and I got progressively nearer the 1989 cuttings. I ate a tuna sandwich at my desk surreptitiously. 'But he's asking for the files on Galileo. It can't be for the *Sun*,' someone complained. 'Why not? We get enough stupid requests about the Spice Girls from the *Sunday Times*, why shouldn't we get Galileo from the *Sun*?' I put my fingers in my ears.

A Dutch TV crew killed in crossfire. 'Weeping nun begs ambassador to halt laughter.' I uncrumpled the headline and found the missing 's'. Ploughing through endless accounts of horror I eventually reached the year in question. The FMLN offensive began in earnest on 11 November 1989 and by the 13th, 197 people had been killed in gun battles in the city, according to the *Daily Mail*. On the 14th the headlines say REBELS TAKE SAN SALVADOR and on the 16th Charles Bremner of *The Times* reports 'At least 650 dead in El Salvador'. I pictured them all sitting in the hotel bar together in the evenings as I had seen them do so many times in Israel and elsewhere. Here we go, I thought.

'*The Times*', *18 November 1989*
A British correspondent was killed yesterday while reporting on the intense fighting between

government forces and left-wing guerrillas in El
Salvador that has left more than 800 dead and 1,000
injured in the past six days . . . He was divorced and
leaves two daughters one of whom is studying
Russian at Oxford . . . Only hours before he was shot
he was telling colleagues that he thought he was
'getting a little too old for this business'.

Shaking and nauseous I turned to the cuttings about Dad.
Lots of them had DEAD written on them in felt-tip. Most
were the obituaries, familiar and benign – written by
Dad's friends, crying into their typewriters.

But the third piece of paper I unfolded contained a
photograph of Dad in the morgue. I stared and stared at it,
trying to take it in. Someone was typing next to me,
insistent and repetitive.

I had been protected from the picture when it graced
the pages of the *Sun* along with some tits and royals scoops
on 18 November 1989. My little sister, Charlotte, saw it
by accident and was deeply disturbed. Used to her dad
being in the States, she couldn't quite make the distinction
between Washington and Dead (I had the same trouble
myself) and she couldn't come to terms with the grotesque
picture of Dad – naked, bloody, casually presided over by
an exhausted pathologist. Samira, her mother, petitioned
the Press Complaints Commission and the *Sun* apologised. Oddly, in 1993 the same paper ran a hysterical campaign about the evil of the man who dared to take and try
to sell photographs of the corpse of soccer legend Matt
Busby.

I hadn't seen my father dead until that day in the
Wapping library. I had thought about him, though. I

thought about him as he was being shipped to London in a plastic bag, and as he was being chopped up by the coroners in King's Cross, and when I saw the seven-foot coffin being carried into the front of the church in Highgate Village.

The forensic scientist who took charge of Dad's body upon its return to London, and whose reports I had seen before leaving for El Salvador, noted that Dad had fallen and hurt his head and right shoulder after he had been shot. Poor Daddy. I sat in a bright London office reading about it. 'Grazing on head. The top button has been torn off the white bloodstained shirt.' My throat was closing and my stomach was leaving its required position – the stains had been photographed up close – but the button thing made me smile through my nausea. I'm sure the button had been twisted off by Dad during a difficult phone conversation, or pulled off by Charlotte, wrapped around his neck, tugging for attention.

'The body is that of a well-nourished Caucasian male.' Well-nourished?! This is the guy who rushed himself into the hospital of Tropical Diseases in King's Cross convinced he had contracted cholera or something far worse in some dusty hell-hole. Mum, Ricky and I had to put sticky labels on cups and forks he had used, keep at least a foot away from him and clean the bath after he had used it, he insisted. 'Too much black coffee, too many cigarettes and not enough to eat.' This was the diagnosis he received after a day of samples and tests. He pulled the sticker off his spoon with a wince of disappointment. He was a pathetic hypochondriac (a hereditary condition, I have discovered) but was never remotely ill that I remember, apart from the chickenpox I gave him when I was thirteen.

The thought of death and illness had him grasping his cigarette all the tighter and he couldn't bear to hear his sister, a cardiac nurse, talk about the patients she had lost that day. Perhaps she and her hi-tech equipment in Albany, New York could have saved him. Saved him and left him paraplegic.

'How old was he?' Dad would ask, nervously swinging on his dinner chair at the news of a fatality. 'Eighty-four,' she might say, and he would sigh, relieved, but saddened by the thought of lonely old age, a heart attack in an unfriendly hospital with all your friends and family already dead. Or, 'Only forty,' she might say and he would twitch into alert mode. 'Christ! Did he smoke? What was the problem?' 'I don't know,' she would laugh. 'A weak heart.' 'Oh, God. Oh Christ,' he would mutter, sucking his smoke in hard.

Well-nourished! 'No, you enjoy your festive Christmas lunch. I'll just go down to Roy Rogers for a lovely burger. Lots of drive-bys this time of year . . .'

One of the photographs showed Dad's face, eyes closed, forehead grazed, very pale, but beautiful and rested, thick brown hair, greying at the temples, coarse and clean. Another showed his whole body from the front. Another from the back. He could have been asleep apart from the crucifix-shaped autopsy scar down the middle of his stomach and across his chest. And the indignity of the position.

I turned the page and caught my breath. The chair seemed to disappear from under me and the room faded into nothingness. I didn't know until then that they shave your head to perform an autopsy. This had been someone so grand and tall that it wasn't until I was about six that I could hold his hand without being lifted off the floor, feet dangling. He could pick you up and put you on his shoulders and you could hardly see the ground. He dipped his cheese in HP sauce and he rocked backwards and forwards in his chair, rubbing his hands on his jeans when he laughed or was saying something funny. And here is where he ended up. On a slab in St Pancras, his lovely thick hair shaven off in clumps, his internal organs God knows where. What was left of them.

I wandered out on to Victoria Street blinded by tears and tried to walk to the tube station. I failed. I sat down by a wall in front of besuited commuters rushing past with briefcases and umbrellas and sobbed into my handbag. His hands had looked so long and white in the photographs. Nails so neat.

For my nerves before going lots of people recommended drugs. I managed to wheedle some diazepam and some betablockers out of my GP and I was planning to take my first dose the night before I left. I carried the brown plastic bottles around in my handbag gleefully, feeling that I had the answer to any potential problem conveniently at hand.

'Aren't betablockers what snooker players take?' said my friend Steve on my last night. 'It stops you shaking but you feel exactly the same inside.'

'God, do you think? I don't know,' I said. I didn't.

'Anyway,' piped up Danny, glancing up from his Café Delancey three-chocolate mousse, 'whatever you do don't take diazepam. It's really bad for you and addictive. I wouldn't touch it.'

Now my hypochondria was overriding my fear of flying off to San Salvador. I was distinctly jittery. Steve decided to change the subject and he gave me my charity. Whenever either of us flies, we give each other money. 'Take this money to San Salvador, via Atlanta, then bring it back and give it to charity,' were my instructions. It is a Jewish thing that Steve got from his uncle. God won't kill you if you're on a charity mission, is the thinking. Unfortunately I am so pathetically superstitious that I can't fly without it now, and Steve and I both fly a lot. We are constantly creeping round to each other's houses in the middle of the night or meeting for some insanely early breakfast just to exchange charity. 'Make sure you always eat a good breakfast,' said Steve before we said goodbye. I promised.

So I was too scared to take my diazepam and when I arrived, quivering, at Heathrow the next morning to get on my flight to Atlanta, I ran into Boots to ask the pharmacist what I should do. Don't take them together, he said. Don't drink with them, he commanded. Just take one of the betablockers. I did. We took off. A state of complete calm and restfulness failed to sweep over me and I couldn't drink away the terror of being on a DC10 too many miles above the sea. The trollies loaded with champagne floated past me unmolested. As we were coming in to land I shut my eyes and clamped my hands over my ears. Then my neighbour tapped me on the arm, pointed out at the friendly, heat-hazy airport coming up to meet the plane and said: 'See, it's OK now.' I relaxed and sat up straight. 'I wouldn't get complacent yet,' I quipped.

The back wheels kissed the runway, the engines roared sickeningly and we swooped vertically back up into the sky. People screamed. I cried. The bloke next to me read the paper as we did the approach again.

Still, it was the first time I have landed anywhere without a hangover since 1985.

Part of the reason for my stopover in Atlanta on the way to Salvador was to be present at my then boyfriend's thirty-fifth birthday party. It was a James Bond party. This, in case you've never attended one, means the men get to wear tuxedos and the women have to look like whores.

It was being held, obviously, by four men. The invitation read: 'The guys are back in search of Octopussy.' Somebody's mother had made a cake in the form of a huge headless, armless, legless female with massive breasts wearing a skimpy orange bikini – everyone's ideal woman.

The party was to be held round a swimming pool in three acres of foresty back garden, and there was a frenzy of kerosene, beer keg and 'food platter' buying preceding the event. The boys in search of Octopussy (without their dinner jackets they might all find it a bit tricky to locate one obliging lady, never mind eight – hence the party, I suppose) traipsed round huge warehouses from hell where you could only buy things in packs of 800. Everyone then drivelled on about how miraculous it was that this very set of 800 paper cups would have cost up to 95 cents more in the outside world. Personally, I would happily have paid $200 for them so as not to have to go into an aircraft hangar full of very fat Americans in shorts waddling round selecting their dream garden furniture.

Anyway, clinging coquettishly to my Pussy Galore hairstyle as we (stupidly) drove a convertible through the Freaknik traffic, we headed off for the party. (For one weekend a year the college students in Atlanta block off the streets with their cars, dance on the bonnets and shout to each other. There were police everywhere and someone, but not necessarily a policeman, threw stones at us from a bridge.)

As the sunset began to colour the sky orange the first forked lightning appeared over the party location. Within the initial half-hour of festivities, I retired, snivelling with pre-Salvador angst that nobody (understandably) was vastly interested in, to a golf cart parked under the porch. A cat came to join me and we sat in humid and contemplative self-pity while the lightning crashed around us and the guests huddled glittering in the distant pool house.

When I finally deigned to emerge, it was the sitting down in the main house drinking cognac stage of things and I poured myself into a soft sofa next to a gorgeous Colombian woman in high heels. 'You OK?' she asked.

'Mmm. Not really,' I wheedled, and told her about where I was going and why. Her eyes lit up as she described an experience she'd had at university in Colombia. She had gone to a kind of political meeting just to see what it was like, and someone was giving a talk about the war in El Salvador. They were shown a video, secretly shot, of some soldiers throwing live babies up in the air on to their bayonets. It was, she said, the most disturbing and appalling thing she had ever seen and it changed her life. It was the first time she had acknowledged that she was part of the Colombian ruling class.

'I had always lived like that,' she said. 'Our house and our whole area was closed off from the poverty and, of course, I would occasionally see the beggars and everything, but I never thought about it until then.'

She could imagine, she explained, how the rich Salvadoreans felt about the war. How it had seemed incomprehensible to many of them and how they would-n't have felt themselves to be doing anything reprehensi-ble in fighting for their lifestyles, or having them fought for.

I drank some more vodka and tried to flirt with a bloke called Amit who had eyelashes like butterfly landing pads. He said he was a pec model. Now I was really on my way.

Marvin seemed to have the whole situation under control. Walkman on, head thrown back, eyes shut, fingers rapping on our shared armrest. I was less relaxed. The crew looked suspiciously tired. If that was the pilot he was far too young, and I was sure I had seen him staggering out of the airport bar earlier while I was tipping down my ninth vodka and tonic to greet the sunrise.

I pretended to look for something in my bag and heaved my elbow in Marvin's somnolent ribs. He opened his huge brown eyes slowly and pulled his headset off to squint more effectively out of the scratched plastic win-dow. He noted that we hadn't taken off yet and shut them again.

'You going home then?' I shouted, hysterically. 'I'm Anna.'

'Yeah,' he smiled, clearly imagining white beaches and azure seas. 'Yeah. Marvin. You?'

'No no. Not me. Uh-uh. Never been to Latin America before actually, but I hear all kinds of good things about it. All that passion. You must be really looking forward to getting there and seeing all your family and everything. Is it far to go from San Salvador for you?' I babbled as the plane heaved, creaked and rattled its trundling way to oblivion.

'Cool,' muttered Marvin as we hurtled past a cloud. I had my eyes shut and my fingers in my ears and had lowered myself as far into my seat as I could. 'Man, you worse than my sister!' I heard him laugh. He'll be laughing on the other side of his face when I drag him from the smouldering wreckage, I thought.

'Buenos días,' somebody chirped over the intercom as we left the world behind. Well, it hadn't been that good so far. My flight from Atlanta to Miami had had no cabin service because the turbulence was so bad, and I had sat sobbing in one of the crew seats while a nice boy called Kai explained the properties of turbulence to me. 'You see? We're in no danger,' he beamed while meal trays fell out of their holes, computers plummeted from overhead lockers and babies screamed their last. 'Mmm-hmm. I see,' I quivered.

This, it had to be admitted, was a lot better. Marvin was joining me in some champagne and giving me a brief course in aeroplane maintenance. Born in El Salvador, he was now a baggage handler for American Airlines in Miami. He was training to be a flight engineer. He spoke with such pride that I imagined someone just like him meticulously checking our mechanical death trap – tightening screws and sticking down Sellotape – and I began to relax.

'So, what takes you to El Salvador?' he asked, once he had satisfied me that triple engine failure was relatively rare and even in the unlikely event of such an emergency we could still glide down safely on to one of those nice mountains over there.

The English, of course, don't allow themselves to express emotions (except mildly ironic interest or distaste) so over the last eight years I have perfected saying the following words in as chirpy a way as possible so as to minimise the potential embarrassment of my interlocutor.

'Actually, my father was shot there in 1989. He was a journalist covering the war. I set off for El Salvador when I heard he'd been shot but I only got as far as Heathrow airport because he died within two hours,' I explained, smiling in a well-you-know-it-could-happen-to-anyone-we-all-have-our-crosses-to-bear kind of way.

We got out our tray tables and Emerita the stewardess put little checked napkins down on them as though we weren't seven miles off the ground in a metal coffin. 'Anyway, I've been meaning to finish that journey for eight years and here I am,' I concluded.

'Unreal,' nodded Marvin, contemplating the bubbles in his champagne. 'My dad was killed there too.'

'Unreal,' I agreed.

And here I was. Eight years late, but on my way at last. Marvin pointed out the volcano through the clouds as we passed it. 'You can see it from everywhere in the city,' he said, glowing with that nearly-there thing that people who genuinely believe the plane will land without bursting into flames get. 'So what's San Salvador like, then?' I asked as the right wing skimmed the crater.

The first thing I'd notice, he said, is the heat. It hits you out of nowhere. 'Apart from that, you know, these days it has McDonald's and Pizza Hut and it's basically like any other city.'

This is a guy, I thought, driving into town an hour later, who hasn't been to Geneva. People in San Salvador are constantly telling you that it's no more dangerous than any other city, that it's just the same as anywhere. This is a lie. The only city in the world to which is might possibly be comparable in terms of violent crime, development and general appearance is Bogota.

Chico met me at the airport and it was, as Marvin had predicted, hot. Chico is helper to an English Jesuit priest called Michael Campbell Johnson who had been recommended to me by everyone who has ever set foot in the country. I had phoned him up from London in a panic about failing to get from the airport to my hotel alive and he had asked Chico to fetch me.

Chico, and everybody else, drives a creaking, rusting old truck with no mirrors, a cracked windscreen and holes in the floor where the road comes in. Pulling my jewellery off as advised brought me out into a bright sweat and I smirked to myself as I opened the window only to find that it made the heat much worse. It was like having a hundred hair-driers aimed at your head. Chico spoke no English. I speak no Spanish (apart from 'Do you like paella? Yes I like it very much'). An impasse.

I asked him if he like paella. I didn't understand his reply, but it wasn't 'Si. Me gusto mucho'.

Watching the ancient Toyota trucks whisk past holding cargoes of shabby men with machine guns squinting into the glare, I reached for my phrase book. 'Muy caliente,' I said, and mimed drinking water. He pulled over at a palm hut where a fat woman with gold teeth was frying tortillas on a black stove. The palm fronds were hanging heavy and still and half-naked men lay immobile under them. The mangoes were too heat-exhausted to cling to the trees any longer and they plopped lethargically into the dust. Chico bought me a Coke and smiled a lot. Waving into the hills he told me (I think) about how his family had been murdered in *el conflicto* and how kind the English padre had been to him and his pregnant girlfriend. Why, he wanted to know (perhaps), was I here?

'Mi padre,' I said, wiping the sweat from my forehead with a shirt sleeve, 'aqui muerte. Periodista. En San Salvador – colonia Mejicanos.' I mimed a sniper taking aim at an unsuspecting journalist. The tortilla woman twitched. Chico shrugged and looked sadly up at the volcano (dark green with jungly-looking trees) and the plant-roofed corrugated iron huts that are dotted about on it.

'No peligroso per me in El Salvador sola?' I asked him. El Salvador is the most dangerous country in the world, with twenty-seven murders a day in its capital city alone out of an overall population of only five million. 'There is significant lawlessness throughout the country,' the Foreign Office had informed me. Chico laughed and looked at me. Blonde, young, no Spanish. 'Si. Peligroso,' he confirmed.

My boiling brain focused on the heat-shimmering chaos of San Salvador as we turned into the city. There was an overwhelming volume of uncontrolled traffic, no shortage of thin-eyed men with AK47s, thick green trees, crumbling colonial buildings withering in the heat, glue-crazed children tapping on the windows with tiny hands and, hey, a drive-thru McDonald's shining idiotically on a street corner against the backdrop of the volcano. Just like anywhere else really. Hampstead in the sun.

We pulled up past the armed security men and in front of the uniformed porters lurking in the shade of the vast

Camino Real hotel. Since I had boarded the plane in Miami with my mouth tasting of hotdog and my eyes red from lack of sleep I had felt myself to be loping along in Dad's shoes. I was even wearing a brown leather jacket and jeans. Here he got on his last plane, had his last mid-air drink with its ice melting against the warm plastic, maybe served by Emerita herself. He smoked his last mid-air cigarette, breaking off the filter and pulling pieces of tobacco off his tongue. Here his fat passport (achingly valid until 1999) was stamped for the last time. He was driven along this airport road never to be driven back. If he had lived he would have returned chatting to the driver, smoking frantically, hoping he would make the plane. And here at the hotel, I was checking in as he had checked in, never to check out.

The thought made me laugh. When I was little and Dad lived in New York he had bought some Roach Motels. They are like big matchboxes and you put them on the floor for cockroaches to crawl into and die. The advert says 'Roach Motel – roaches check in . . . but they *don't* check out.' Dad used to love saying it and I was muttering it to myself as I handed my credit card to Hector, head concierge at the Camino Real. 'Room 617, Meees Blundy.'

I was so glad to have got there alive that I gave five dollars to the bell-boy who spoke perfect English, probably had a degree in modern languages and whose two brothers had died in the war. I wanted it to seem momentous, this hotel whose name had always carried a portent of death. 'Camino Real', I felt, ought to be scrawled in bloodied Gothic letters over the entrance. The concierge ought to have been a wizened hunchback, not a charming

caballero. I wanted to find a scrap of paper with Dad's
handwriting on it or to see commemorative photographs
of hotel staff murdered in the conflict, but it was just a
hotel – mini-bar, CNN, white towels and club sandwiches on the room service menus.

'Gracias,' I said to Roberto who was adjusting the air
conditioning.

'Sure. Let me know if you need anything else, ma'am,'
he smiled.

I stared out of the window. After all those years of waiting for you at home I've traipsed out here to find you at
last and you're not here, I thought.

When my mother and I lived in a flat on a main road I
would sit in the window counting the cars going past until
Dad came. Sometimes he was hours or days late. At first I
would be angry that he had forgotten, then terrified that
something had happened to him, then angry again as news
item after news item bore no sign of an air crash.
Ultimately I would be relieved and grudgingly elated.

Even when I was eighteen I was pleading with him to
come home and see me.

Oxford, 1989
Am very tired, have had no sleep 'cos of that stupid
essay which is actually quite good – the only decent
one I've written since I got here, but my tutor hasn't
heard it yet. If it takes twelve hours to write a good
essay, I don't think I'll be bothering again. I notice
that President Bush is looking considerably older than
he did last time I dined with him – at the Jefferson in
'82. When are you coming over? (Don't bother). Be

here for my birthday if you come at all. Anyway, it's your turn to write, pig features.

Lots of Love, Anna.

I was slightly more honest a decade or so earlier.

London, circa 1976
dear daddy

I wish you were coming back now but you aer not coming back now. thank you for the hippopotamus and the doll. i miss you very much daddy. i haven't been swimming for a long time.

luv from anna

That card was sent with a felt-tip drawing at the bottom of myself and Mum going shopping at Budgen's. Dad was terrified of suburban life, family life – it appalled him and he laughed fondly at our shopping trips, what I was doing at school, my crushes on ludicrous pop stars of whom he hadn't heard (Adam Ant and then Boy George. We can't all have our sexuality under control) and what he must have seen as the cosy mundanity of our life. After all, where he was people were dying, governments were being overthrown, world-famous luminaries were making decisions that affected the lives of millions – really important things were happening.

When I started going out with Giles Coren, aged eighteen, Dad turned up in London on his way home to America after the Reagan-Gorbachev summit in Helsinki. It was a surprise visit and it meant I had to cancel a few meetings with Giles. 'Some boyfriends have other men to compete with – I have to contend with the whims of

Superpowers,' he said. Even now I am idiotically blasé about the schedules of world leaders or former leaders dictating my diary – someone actually called me about eight seconds ago to tell me Gorbachev had a sore throat so could we move dinner to Saturday?

The fact that I had schoolfriends and cared about whether or not they liked me seemed quaint and hilarious to Dad as the world rumbled, and even now I cringe with embarrassment at the picture I drew and how homely and tedious that life might have seemed to him.

Diary, 6 October 1982: Dad came home with a cotton plant from the Garden of Eden.

How could you compete with the dream-like unreality of that kind of thing?

I found myself ludicrous as I saw me through his eyes and I felt boring and unglamorous, understanding that he would rather be sitting in a desert tent at a suicide bomber trainee camp than coming to Budgen's with us. So would I, I thought, if I had the choice. And he would forever translate the danger and unpredictability of life in Beirut or Tripoli to Crouch End, infecting me with fear that the paddling pool in Priory Park might explode in flames at any minute or that gunmen lurked on the roof of my school.

Once we were walking up Fifth Avenue in New York. We passed a phone booth just opposite the Metropolitan Museum of Art and called my mum in England. I called her incessantly from everywhere, hoping that things were at least safe somewhere. Every time he passed it from then on he would call me. 'Guess where I am?' he would shout above the police sirens. 'Our phone box?' I would guess, or sometimes I would pretend not to know. He hated that. 'No! Go on! Guess again!' he shouted, hurt. Anyway, there we were and I was probably nine or so.

'What would you do if someone opened fire on us now?' he asked as we walked through the thick heat. I said I would run into a shop. 'No,' he said, quite serious. He said I should lie on the floor immediately. If I was passing a shop window that I could jump through to lie flat for extra protection, fine, but if not I should just lie down. I still think about it, and I do get a bit edgy walking between brick walls. If there is a bomb, lie with your feet in the direction of the explosion.

I started to believe that life was as precarious as he suggested and I was bored and almost disappointed that mine wasn't. I knew why he did his job. Who wouldn't? I thought. Far more fun to be chewing on a sheep's eyeball or sleeping with a beautiful local girl (or both) than to turn up on Priory Road in the rain at a flat opposite the fire station. We were enchanted when he did. Well, I was. Mum took the piss out of him, but was pleased to see him nonetheless.

'Make me a cup of coffee, wife!' he declared, draping a leg across the arm of the sofa and slumping back with his eyes shut.

'Not wife any more, actually. We're divorced.'

'Are we?' His eyes flashed open. 'Oh. Well, make me one anyway,' he concluded, shutting them again.

When I was tiny (three or four) I wrote a book about my dad on thick khaki school paper. 'My Dad' it says on the front in blue crayon. 'My Dab is big,' reads the first page and there is a drawing of a huge stick man with long black hair. 'My Dab takes me for a ride,' page two. A big person and a smaller person close together in a blue circle, arms like ski poles. Page four is in black crayon. 'MY DAD goes in an aeroplane,' it says, and shows what looks like a Tiger Moth with one face in the cockpit. 'MY DAD,' explains the last page, 'switches the light on.'

And here, I thought, the light was finally switched off.

I paced around the Camino Real room a bit, peering into the wardrobes, doing a mini-bar inventory, smelling the soaps and shampoos and rifling through Revelations in my Gideons Bible. The television had forty-seven channels and I found the one with *Are You Being Served?* on it and listened to Mrs Slocombe making hilarious quips about her pussy while I looked out at the view. The sky behind the hills was beginning to blush pink and the neon around the city had flickered into action. Across the street was the biggest (and perhaps only) shopping mall in San Salvador – Metrocentro.

It is apparently *the* place to go girl watching. 'Yes, but have you actually scored there?' I asked the lech who had made the claim. 'Fuck yeah!' he replied.

People were streaming out of it with bags in their hands and on their heads. Children were selling Kleenex and tortillas to the rich shoppers and yellow taxis were hustling for clients. Overflowing buses stopped outside and ragged teenagers leapt out shouting destinations and cajoling people into boarding in a way that looked far more like an arm-waving, barefooted, tooth-baring threat than an invitation.

I asked somebody later what had happened to all the government troops who had committed atrocities during the civil war and who had been pardoned in the peace agreement. 'They became bus drivers,' I was told. It is claimed that most of these bus drivers have a deal with one or other local gang or *mara* (the main ones of which are organised from Los Angeles and Miami) which involves allowing *mara* members to board their vehicle, rob everyone and get off again with the minimum possible violence. 'Don't travel by bus,' I had been warned. Well, I try not to do *that* in London.

As the light outside turned to a thin silhouette of blue over the darkening mountains and Captain Peacock was receiving his come-uppance, I took to the shower and watched the Atlanta, Miami and El Salvador dust and sweat trickle through my newly painted toes. (Darlene, a veteran of Nail City in Atlanta's glitziest mall, had recommended cherry red.) It was time to make my phone calls.

I had called journalist Tom Long from the States and explained who I was and why I was coming to Salvador. He had covered the whole conflict in El Salvador from its beginnings in the late 1970s to the 1992 peace agreement. At one time he had fought for his patch as the world's press gleefully packed the bar at the Camino Real and the television correspondents did their pieces to camera in front of the dense foliage by the pool – looks just like a jungle if you frame it right. Now Tom is one of the only western journalists in the country and he is everybody's correspondent there. 'I'm really glad you called,' he told me, because he had a theory about my father's murder which nobody had ever looked into before. He had been meaning to mention it for years. 'Yeah, I was in that district, in Mejicanos, the day before your dad was killed, on the 16th of November,' he said. He had a story that he would tell me when I arrived.

Even as he said it, crackling into the receiver so casually while I sat in a pristine, suburban American kitchen, it was a jolt. A thunderstorm had turned the Atlanta sky dark green outside and a vase of thirty-five pink roses I had bought as a birthday present stood on the table in front of me. I was listening to the voice of this man who had actually been there when my father was killed. He remembered. He could show me the spot. 'I might be out by about ten yards, but you know . . .' Suddenly, I understood that it had really happened. I have always felt vaguely as though it was some self-indulgent story I had made up to make my life sound more glamorous.

I reached for the phone and dialled Tom's number.

Chapter Three

He past; a soul of nobler tone:
My spirit loved and loves him yet,
Like some poor girl whose heart is set
On one whose rank exceeds her own.

He mixing with his proper sphere,
She finds the baseness of her lot;
Half jealous of she knows not what,
And envying all that meet him there.

So many times on so many nights I had heard the phone
ring from my room at the top of my mother's house in
Crouch End. Never able to sleep very well, I looked out
at my three stars (I later found out they make up Orion's
belt), and listened out for the rings. They never come if
you wait for them – I got into phone watching earlier than
other girls – but the moment you drop off . . .

I would pad out of my room in the dark, warm with
sleep and smiling to myself, indulgent and already forgiv-
ing. 'Yeah? Whaddya want?' I said, fondly. 'It's the middle
of the night.'

'Not here it's not. It's early evening/mid-afternoon/
dawn/lunchtime. Anyway, can't you spare a few
moments to talk to your old Daddikins?' he would whine.
I was huddled on the floor, the orange glow of the street
lamps lighting the figures of Mum and Ricky like sleeping

seals in the bed. 'Some people are trying to get a bit of shut-eye,' Ricky might murmur. 'Enough now,' Mum occasionally said.

'Well, I'm not there, am I? I'm here and no I can't . . . Is it hot?' I asked, if I could hear those sireny, trafficky noises of hot places.

'Hot?! You could fry an egg on the bonnet of a car!' he would begin. We tried this once by the Dead Sea. It went a bit white round the edges but didn't cook, which was surprising because breathing was like having boiling oil poured down your throat.

He would tell me who in the press pack was in the hotel and insisted I knew them all by their ridiculous nicknames alone, although I could never remember having met them.

'You *do* know! He was at that wedding/You were sick in his car/She gave you that doll/He stole my suit.' He told me who was illicitly sharing a room with whom even before I was old enough to quite grasp the significance of this. (I love meeting the protagonists now.)

He described the scene down in the hotel bar and the jokes they had told. He taught me bits of Arabic and explained the political situation of wherever he might be. 'So there was this bloke, Paul Lighterfuel . . .' he said.

'Funny name. Paul Lighterfuel,' I mumbled, half asleep.

'No! No! He *poured* lighter fuel all over the table and . . .' he went on, irritated that I might not be interested, desperate to keep my attention.

I was always flattered that he had called, like a mother waiting for a word from her errant son – pathetically grateful when it came. But now that I do quite a lot of traipsing around the world myself, staying in strange hotels, forging artificially close friendships fast, and illicitly moving rooms at night, I have realised that he was lonely and glad to have someone who was always waiting for him on the other side of world, always pleased to hear from him and always there to listen to his stories in the middle of the night when the whisky was finished.

I never know who to call, myself. Should I wake up so-and-so? Will he think I'm a psychopath? Of course, if he were still alive, I'd call Dad. Pay him back for all my years of hoping the phone would ring in the night. 'Hi! I'm in Moscow. It's so cold your spit freezes before it hits the ground. Meier's here – you *do* know him! I was at Oxford with him . . .'

I used to feel so sorry for Dad when he said he had had dinner in the hotel alone or gone to a restaurant alone or sat in an airport waiting, frustrated, for a delayed plane. 'But I don't mind at all. I read the papers. It's better than being with someone you hate,' he would say and I didn't believe him. I thought the worst thing in the world was to be alone somewhere weird. But now I can sit at an Italian restaurant on the patio of the Nile Hilton, reading and writing notes to myself in the back of my book, drinking wine and smoking shisha, and I desperately hope that nobody will come and talk to me. Now I know what he meant.

Now I know what he meant about lots of things.

But perhaps unlike most wandering journalists Dad always had someone to send postcards to – to chart his progress and register his experiences. If you contact some-one from Timbuktu it proves you were there, no matter how short your trip or how bad your hangover. A cure for existential angst.

His mild desperation and loosely rational fear of impending disaster completely infected my life. The first diary I ever wrote begins with a list of things I can remember. It runs: I broke a glass, the sink fell off, the cabinet fell down, Sammy the dog died, a boy was sick in his food at nursery school, the lightbulb exploded, Adrian Gore died, I had a balloon but it blew away.

As I got older I would headline my entries with events Dad was embroiled in – *January 18th 1981 Hostages Released* – and then go on to describe the more banal details of my life at home.

All these postcards he sent me, all his little messages were weighed down with various kinds of angst.

Boston 1976
Dear Anna

Thank you very much for your letter and your pictures. They were all very nice. I particularly liked the one about the disappearing house. I'm glad my house doesn't disappear. If it did then I wouldn't be able to go to bed or have a cup of tea. Mind you, if I disappeared as well then it wouldn't matter much if the house disappeared . . . I'm sorry I won't be back for Christmas. Nancy (you talked to her on the phone) has bought an enormous Christmas tree – about ten feet high – and put it in the lounge. It has hundreds of lights on it which flash on and off. You would like it. Next Christmas we'll get an even bigger one for Priory Road or wherever we happen to be.

I've been writing a story about an American policeman – an FBI man and I have to follow him everywhere he goes. He has a big car with a telephone in it, a blue flashing light (like that Kojak) and a siren that goes Wheeeeeeeee when he turns it on. He also has a gun but he doesn't shoot anyone with it. Not me anyway. He is called Bill. Ruth [my mum] – Halina looked nice. I will marry her. How much does she earn? Miss you very much. Love Daddy. xxxxxxxxxxxxxxxxxxxxxxxxxxxxxxxxxxxxxxx

New York, 1976: The New York Skyline: Dear Gleamer, well here I still am in New York. I'm at Kennedy Airport which is very big waiting to fly to somewhere called Los Angeles. My shoe leaks and my foot is damp. Also my head is a bit hot. I took a picture of one of those sky scrapers this morning but it was so big I couldn't get it all in. I don't think you'd like New York. No paddling pools. Love Daddy.

Morocco, 1981: Some Camels: Dear Miss Blundy. I am in Morocco after a personal invitation to the King's birthday. Very nice. He had a seven foot high birthday cake. I haven't phoned because I have been in the middle of the bleeding desert and they didn't have any. It is very cold. Why am I here? Daddikins.

Morocco was the one place he conceded he had vaguely liked in his leaving letter to the *Sunday Times*. 'I will miss the Middle East,' he wrote, '(with the exception of Iraq, Jordan, Libya, Sudan, Israel and West Beirut – Morocco was all right) but I know that I have left it in more slender and probably more competent hands than my own.'

Haiti, 1979: PRO ANNA BLUNDY EX PRINCE OF

DARKNESS AND KING OF ALL EVIL PORT AU PRINCE
HAITI THANK YOU FOR YOUR ENQUIRY RE
CASTING GHASTLY SPELLS ON A CERTAIN MR
PARNELL [my form teacher] I THINK I HAVE ENOUGH
DATA TO GO AHEAD NOW AND THE HIDEOUS
RITUAL HAS BEEN PREPARED. I SHALL UPDATE YOU
ON DEVELOPMENTS. THANKS A LOT FOR YOUR
HELP WITH THE GHASTLY SPELL ON THE
INTERNATIONAL MONETARY FUND IN
WASHINGTON. HOPE YOU CAN BE OF HELP WHEN
YOU RETURN TO ENGLAND HEH HEH HEH WARM
REGARDS PRINCE OF DARKNESS KING OF ETC
ENDIT.

By the mid-Eighties I felt ridiculously bourgeois reading these missives over Alpen and coffee in my pink and white striped summer uniform, feeling for my fags in the zip-up pocket before going out to the W3 bus stop in the yellow dawn light.

Sudan, 1984: Dear Anna, have had my hair cut at 'Scowls' of Khartoum like the lady front top right. Cost 3p. Just had a dust sandwich for tea. Very nice. Much cooler in the evening, it goes down to 97 degrees. If you sent your egg over I might be able to fry it on fevered brow. Must go now as there is another chat show about interpretations of the Koran on TV. Mustn't miss it.

Libya 1985: Arrogant, barbaric, savage, frivolous, stray running piglet of imperialism.

44

He liked it best when he was writing or talking to me about somewhere I had been or could imagine. If I didn't know anything about the country he was in, he would describe it in great detail, and if I went somewhere to visit him he would take me to every bar he had been to and introduce me to every last person he knew so that when he called me the next time I could place him better.

1982

That summer when I was twelve, I flew out to Jerusalem.

I went El Al and they spent hours going through my stuff at Heathrow, prodding the life out of Bernard, my bear, and opening all the bottles in my wash bag. I went everywhere with Bernard, a lugubrious-looking St Bernard dog bought for me on a nocturnal drive between New York and Washington, during which I had sat seething and nauseous in the back of the car. 'I'll buy him for you if you promise to stop moaning,' said Dad at the service station, notorious, he claimed, for drive-by shootings. I promised. I lied.

What with Dad's obsession with them, I had a heightened awareness of terrorist activists and suspected everyone else in the queue (obviously guilty as sin). I had my instructions for ideal behaviour in the event of a hijacking and knew to make sure nobody stamped my passport in Tel Aviv. It was the first time I wasn't flying 'unaccompanied' like I usually did to America, so there was no special help or attention, nobody giving me plastic bags full of pencils and badges and nobody patronising me in a way I had of course absolutely despised since I was eight.

I sat in the departure lounge and painted my nails in a colour called 'rose tea'. The lady I had sat next to on my flight to New York the summer before had recommended it to me and I subsequently wheedled a bottle out of my seething father. 'I don't see why you have to wear revolting nail varnish. Does your mother let you, and if so why?' 'Yes and because I want to,' I replied, threatening a scene.

At Tel Aviv there was nobody there to meet me. Dad is easy to spot in an airport because he towers above everyone else (I often think I see him still). I peered around. I was wearing a red, yellow and black flowery dress that had a white nylon cord round the waist, brown sandals and a straw hat with a red band. It was fantastically hot and my bag was heavy. I was swept along in the crowd of people heading for the exit and the sun outside was blinding magnesium white. The only palm trees I had ever seen were the neat, manicured, boulevard palm trees of America and these were different – random, taller and planted in red dust. The only guns I had come across so far were in the holsters of huge-thighed and smiling traffic cops, but here there were teenage soldiers everywhere holding machine guns in a way that suggested they might start firing at any moment should the urge take them. I stood there on my own staring out at the motorways in the dust and wondering what to do.

Someone kicked my case from behind. 'Khilloo leeetle girl. Dees vay,' said Dad, grabbing my bag and hustling off into the maze of cars.

The American Colony Hotel in Jerusalem had an entrance that seemed like a hole in the wall. The sandy streets were deserted apart from a few small boys with donkeys, and the darkening air was singing with crickets and scented with lemons. The reception area had hanging brass lamps and a vast and imposing concierge with amazingly large hands.

'Ahlan, ahlan,' he said, and I loved it. It was the first time I had heard real Arabic and it sounded like a thrilling whisper – insidious secrets being communicated under the breath. I saw a lizard run across the tiled floor and nobody paid attention to it but me. I was almost faint in the heat and my shoes hurt.

Dad took the heavy key and led me down whitewashed stone corridors to my room at the top of a tower. I wasn't to drink the water and I had my own flask of chilled mineral water, long before you got that kind of thing routinely in England. Dad was going down to the bar so I put my nightdress on, brushed my teeth with the water from the flask and got into the crisp, starched sheets in my circular room in the minaret. I lay back and found the three stars in Orion's belt as the muezzin started to sing above the traffic and the insects into the thick night. I read a chapter of a book called *Codename Icarus* that had an orange cover, settled Bernard in and went to sleep.

In the morning I was first up in the whole hotel so I ordered myself breakfast under the lemon trees in the courtyard and did the Jumble and anagrams game in the *International Herald Tribune*. This type of behaviour earned me a reputation as precocious, but I certainly wasn't stupid enough to try and rouse a Mogadonned Dad at this hour. I got white rolls, ham and a cheese I didn't recognise from the buffet. There were peaches and mangoes in piles but I didn't dare disturb them. The waiter with big hands poured me coffee from a huge brass pot and put slices of lemon on a plate beside my cup. Lizards crept across the cobbles to find patches of sun in the dappled light that filtered through the heavily laden trees.

As I scribbled my final answer into the prescribed boxes next to the cartoons – The heavyweight champion's prize possession? A 'd-e-f-t-l-e-f-t' – the hacks began to emerge, with red, puffy eyes, shaking fingers and squashed cigarette packets. 'Morning!' I shouted brightly to the ones I knew. They winced. Some French TV correspondent kept doing pieces to camera from his table, presumably cutting the shot off just above his coffee cup.

Dad took me around the Old City where wrinkled hags sold Ugli fruit from their laps, wizened men in head-dresses pulled donkeys on ropes, boys in rags carried vast plates of couscous on their heads, swaggering men in robes drank tiny cups of coffee and smoked bubbling pipes in alcoves, and women in veils made their cacophonous way round the swarming stalls. 'If anybody starts shooting, lie on the floor,' said Dad. Nobody did and I bought a miniature brass coffee set for Mum, a head-dress for Ricky and I wasn't allowed an Ugli fruit.

We watched people bang their heads against the Wailing Wall and Dad explained to me how it was possible to gauge the level of someone's religious orthodoxy by the extent of the seriousness of their facial expression. The very orthodox Hasids we called 'Hmmmmmmmmmms', putting on an imitation grimace, forlorn and disapproving tone as though we were the headmaster of a school at which all the pupils had turned out to be pornographers and heroin addicts. For the people with beards and skull-caps we would turn down our mouths and 'hmmmmmm', as though unsure of our Latin verb endings, and for those Israelis dressed like American teenagers we would smile and say 'hmm', like we'd forgotten to get the milk at the supermarket but we didn't really need any anyway.

'Is he hmmmmmmmmmmmm, hmmmmmm or hmm?' I would ask when Dad went to interview anyone Israeli.

In the evenings Dad's girlfriend, Shirley, liked to go jogging and we would follow her up hills in the beige Volvo, watching her yellow satin shorts flap up and down in front of the crawling car. I stood on top of the Mount of Olives and sang *The Sound of Music* to the fuzzy pastelled sunset.

One day we went out to the West Bank to visit Dad's fixer and I was forbidden from eating anything in case I caught amoebas. Mohammed's mum, whose head-dress had tinkling coins round the front, was serving delicious-looking delicacies ('Don't be stupid. It's some old goat's eye'). She fetched them from her stove above where the animals were kept and Dad, I noticed, was stuffing them down and cheerfully swilling mint tea. We sat outdoors (in fact the house didn't have an indoors to speak of) and I went into the grove at the back with the fixer to pick grapes and olives from the grey trees. It was very hot. I developed a crush on this fixer who wore maroon loafers and white socks and had reflector shades. He was probably about twenty.

A huge crowd of ragged, grinning children ran in from the village to look at my hair, which was long and blonde. I let them all touch it one by one and they giggled and let me hold a little yellow chick they had brought with them.

But most days at the American Colony were spent by the pool with the tabloid hacks while Dad went out investigating. My companions would listen to the BBC World Service and rush upstairs to file copy when anything salient was announced. The lifeguard, Mohammed,

taught me the Arabic I'm still using today. 'Hello. Hi.
Thank you. Thank you very much. How are you? Fine.
So so. Shit. Enough.' It never fails me. After I had left he
wrote me a letter telling me he loved me.

I read my book, got a serious tan for the first time and
swam a lot.

> **Diary, Monday 16 August 1982:** Got up at 7.30
> and went for a cold swim with a gay bloke here called
> Graham. He's nice. Got Dad and Shirley up and ate
> breakfast. Dad sat there for hours reading the papers
> and talking to the other journalists. I was bored. Then
> we all went to lots of travel agents all of whom were
> Israeli and said 'Shalom'. Dad tied Shirley's laces
> together.

This was the day before the night we went to Lebanon.
We had to leave at 4a.m., so I retired to bed at six in the
evening to ensure a good night's sleep. The others
decided to stay up. 'Lovely day!' I chirped into the darkness at a specially laid on breakfast. Nobody answered me.
Nobody looked well. We piled into two cars, one of
which Dad was driving. I had to sit in the back although
everyone knew I got carsick. I sulked. I can still see and
feel the black plastic mats on the car floor and smell the
cigarette smoke generated by five hungover, chain-
smoking foreign correspondents. I wore my straw hat.

> **Diary, Tuesday, 17 August 1982:** Was called at
> 3.30 and got ready and did final packing. Hotel dark.
> Got Dad and Shirley up and we (and Phil, Bill,
> Ancient Hugh and Mrs Ancient) ate a prepared cold

breakfast. Me being the only one who'd slept. Drove to Tiberius through the border with Dad's press card and watched the sun rise. Got out once and frizzled. 115 degrees. Could barely breathe. Silent and horrid. Lovely. Arrived at a sleazy three star motel on the Sea of Galilee. Dad and the rest left, Shirley slept so Mrs Ancient and I walked around, swam in the lovely freshwater, choppy sea/lake. Mmm. Read a lot and got burnt. Dad came back and we all mucked about with the other journalists. Dinner at a Chinese restaurant. Had a HUGE row but he apologised. Am reading *Innocent Blood* by PD James.

On that desert drive the roads seemed sometimes to run out and the drivers raced each other across the sand which flew up the sides of the car. The desert rippled gold into the distance all around and the sky exploded into fiery colour out of the darkness without any sort of warning, making everything glint and sparkle as women appeared out of nowhere with jugs on their shoulders, walking barefoot to the wells.

I stayed in a kibbutz on the border with Lebanon and spent the days swimming and writing my diary while the men went off being manly. I made friends with a cocker spaniel who lived by the dining room doors. Fighter planes roared overhead in convoy at regular intervals and wounded Israeli soldiers were occasionally brought in on stretchers. 'It was fucking ghastly,' Dad told me while a Duran Duran video from a TV hoisted up to the ceiling distracted me ('Rio'). 'He didn't have his safety catch on and he just shot his friend in the next seat.' He gave me the dead boy's gun holster, which I still have. I had a crush on the guy who scrubbed the floors in the corridors.

Throughout his time in the Middle East, Dad would insist I must remember every single drunk I met on this trip. 'Oh, come *on*! He was sitting in the back of that other car. When we stopped at Lake Tiberius he got his hand stuck in the window winder.' Oh of course, him. All I remembered was being persistently carsick.

1974

And if I wasn't carsick I was alien-house-sick. Every time I went to this place in Clapham that he shared with a woman called Sue I felt sick, or pretended to feel sick. I wet the bed routinely and Dad – whose bed I had to sleep in until he and whoever wanted to go to sleep: then I would be woken and moved – would wake me up and take me to the loo at regular intervals. In theory I would then be moved to the sofa or wherever it was I was supposed to be sleeping, but I think I usually got scared and couldn't get back to sleep again, so I would feel sick (either really or, as Dad tended to argue, psychosomatically) and demand to be taken home to Mum. I hated being so far from home in a flat where I didn't have a room and with someone so glaringly unreliable.

Psychosomatic was a big word with Dad. He was forever telling me that my carsickness was invented (my terror of leaving the safety of Mum for God knows what), and my fear of flying and my refusal to go on roller-coasters.

> 1988: By the way you know your absurd and irritating fear of flying for which you certainly get not a jot of sympathy from me – it is odd that since you

mentioned it almost all the passengers on flights
originating in the US have been sucked out when
large holes appear in the fuselage. It is not worrying of
course, but vaguely disconcerting. It is very nice
travelling in first class with terrific food and fine wine,
the problem is that you normally get sucked out
before you can eat it. Six people were sucked out
yesterday. Still, nothing to worry about.

So I sat in the back of the car, flew and went on roller-
coasters. He seemed not to realise that the sickness and
fear is no less real for being psychologically induced.

I don't know how many times this actually happened,
but I remember watching the orange street lamps flash
above my head as I was rushed back to Crouch End in the
car and I can recall feeling comforted when we crossed
Suicide Bridge near Archway – something I recognised.
Clapham seemed unimaginably far away from Crouch
End and I resented the car journey and the experience as
a whole once I arrived. I still loathe South London today
and I don't imagine it often being daytime there.

Chapter Four

Strange friend, past, present, and to be,
Loved deeplier, darklier understood;
Behold I dream a dream of good
And mingle all the world with thee.

1997
I recognised Tom in the Camino Real's sparkling lobby as
though he were a member of my family. He looked like a
raddled, cynical, brain-fried, emotionally damaged and
permanently lost foreign correspondent. Too long in the
direct sunlight, too much time plumbing the depths of
humanity, too much to drink. These are the people I grew
up with. I like them. They never think I am unstable or
ridiculous. I can relax with them and they nod sagely and
smile.

I have sat around poker tables tugging at Dad's shirt
sleeves, wanting to go to bed and watching these people,
who were miles away from their families if they had them
and who were desperate for another whisky so they didn't
have to go to bed on their own just yet.

'Hey,' said Tom, shaking my hand and gesturing to his
car outside. I say car. It was a vast beaten-up and grimac-
ing jeep as old as the civil war. I had to crawl in the
driver's side because the passenger door had been bashed
in. The gleaming doormen smirked. 'I hate this hotel,'
spat Tom, who, it transpired, hates everything. 'They're

all working for the government. *He's* OK though. Used to smoke joints with me on the second floor,' he laughed, slapping hands with a porter who was just heaving a white man's bags on to his brass trolley.

Tom's post-apocalyptic machine choked out of the drive and straight into four lanes of blazing oncoming traffic. 'Now that's what's scary about this place,' he laughed, screeching into second gear as a shoeless cigarette vendor in a baseball cap leapt backwards on to the pavement. The heat and dust of the night crept in through the broken window and it occurred to me that dangerous driving wasn't really what was scary about this place.

'Are there really murders all the time?' I asked, looking at the black-clad petrol station security guard who was waving his rifle idly.

'Yeah,' said Tom. 'But it's a numbers game. You don't want to worry about it.' Then again, Tom didn't look like a guy who wanted to worry about much. Therefore I took the responsibility upon myself and bit at the skin around my thumbnail. We drove around dark backstreets lined with low shady houses and huge menacing trees. 'Why do they paint the bottoms of the trees white?' I wanted to know.

'The ants. You know? Leafcutter ants. It's crazy shit. They can denude a tree like that in minutes. It's great to watch.' There was something about the way he said 'denude' that I didn't quite like.

We lurched to a stop on a dark deserted pavement. I could hear insects and distant traffic and it was hot. 'Just wanna get a friend of mine. His dad died here too. You'll have a lot in common.' Oh, superb. It seems to be all the rage in this place. I feel an Oscar Wilde quote coming on.

We stepped up on to a black porch under a dense low-hanging mango tree that obscured the house. Tom rang. The door opened and a mango plopped on to the step, tearing its skin. 'Hey,' said a young blond surfer type. 'I'll join you guys in a minute, man,' he drawled and shut the door. This was Eros Kropotkin Hoagland.

His father, *Newsweek* photographer John Hoagland, had been shot in the back by government troops on 16 March 1984 while fourteen-year-old Eros, back in California, was getting ready to play a game of lacrosse. A photographer himself (no surprises), Hoagland junior came to El Salvador in 1996 to see where his father died and he had been unable to tear himself away – the surfing, the Salvadoreans. He describes himself as 'a carbon copy' of his father, another glamorously unattainable figure whose death only served to make him more of a revered enigma to the child left behind. Eros would sneer at this analysis, but we have both been dumped with the spectre of men, widely considered so wonderful that we can only ever fail by comparison, should comparison be drawn. And it is, if only by ourselves.

And here we were in some Salvadorean bar, grim and ironic the three of us, Tom, Eros and I, hot and drunk and finding no comfort in each other's presence.

La Ventana is run by a war-weary German guy who had strong FMLN connections during the conflict. Ventana is whitewashed and opens on to the pitch-dark street. It has local art on the walls and cool, low ceilings. Tom ordered a beer and tapped his cigarette on the table to pack the tobacco down. He muttered something to a boy with a shaven head and black nail varnish (the drummer for a band called Adrenaline, it turned out) and pointed at a waitress.

'I knew it!' he exclaimed excitedly and called her over.

She didn't seem insanely keen to come but she hugged him anyway and laughed at whatever he said before abruptly taking our order.

'Man, she has changed so much,' sighed Tom, lighting his cigarette. 'Last time I saw her she was a guerrilla up in the mountains. She was queen of the mountain, man. She had this long hair and a violet ribbon round her AK47 for Women's Day.' He laughed wryly. 'She was really diggin' that status.'

The journalists miss the war.

Eros told me that his father was at one stage number 30 on a death squad hit list and had a T-shirt made with a 30 on it in the centre of a target. Grim press-pack humour that I suppose was designed to hide the fear with machismo. 'He was a revolutionary,' said Eros proudly. 'What he did mattered. He believed in this shit.'

The brutality of the whole thing was unimaginable. Journalists who covered it tell you about the piles of heads, corpses dumped into the volcano, unrecognisable torture victims. On 22 February 1981 the *Sunday Times* ran a piece by my father that included the story of Lolita who lay, shot fifteen times by government troops, in the Sumpul river while her three children were dying in her arms of gunshot wounds. 'That night she felt an object bump against her in the river. Then it floated off downstream. It was, she says, the head of a child. The next morning a Honduran fisherman pulled in his nets. They contained the bodies of three dismembered children.' Lolita lived through the Sumpul river massacre, and I wonder if she survived the war.

Eros, Tom and I were soon joined at La Ventana by a fat Salvadorean who had spotted us from across the bar. He smoked cigars that he kept in a leather case and lit them with a heavy silver lighter. He perched on his stool and listened to the conversation until Tom invited him in. 'This is Anna. Her dad was shot in the November offensive. The day after the priests. Remember?' What an introduction. Everyone is Salvador is so desensitised to violence that I think they imagine that you give as little a toss about your own father's death as they do. Fat Man drew on his cigar and stared through the waitress. 'Yeah. How'ya doing?' he asked me. He turned out to be a photographer and said he had been in the Rosales hospital where my father died on the day they brought him in.

Something hideous and snakes-in-the-stomach-producing occurred to me. I smiled at Fat Man and felt myself going a bit pale, the alcohol draining depressingly out of me.

'Did you take a photograph of my father on the slab in the morgue?' I asked as though with polite interest. As if to say: 'Oh yes. You must have taken that wonderful still life of an egg in an elbow?' He nodded in a self-deprecating way. After all, he didn't like to boast but now I mentioned it that was, as it happened, an *oeuvre* of his.

I took a sip of my wine and could feel the wicker of the stool pressing against me as every muscle tensed in my effort to keep smiling and not tear the cigar from this guy's mouth and shove it down his throat. 'Wow! I've always wondered who took that,' I chirped. 'You sold it to the *Sun*, right?'

He had indeed proffered his work to that fine British institution and received pecuniary recompense for his efforts. 'How much did they pay you, Alex?' (for he did, in fact, have a name). I said this as though it were a hilarious jape and I was cheekily pushing my luck.

'Not enough!' he cackled, nearly rolling off his seat.

We all broke out laughing loudly. There was no controlling my mirth.

Tom drove me home and I lay blankly on my king-size bed watching films dubbed into Spanish on HBO Olé.

Tom Long had agreed to take me to Mejicanos where my dad 'bought it', but he couldn't go the next day. He drew a map on a napkin of the crossroads where it happened – an X marked where Dad had fallen. 'The government was losing ground all over the place that day. They were terrified and shooting at anything,' he laughed. 'That was the best week of the whole thing, man. We were having a great time.' I couldn't imagine why he had said that and, judging by his immediate glance down at the wet napkin tied around his beer bottle, neither could he. We agreed to go two days later on a Friday.

So the next morning I took my hangover downstairs in the mirrored lift ('Buenos días, Mees Blundy') for lunch with Father Michael Campbell Johnson.

He is the Jesuit who had arranged for me to be picked up at the airport. He was tanned, bearded, shambolic and wore an old T-shirt and sandals – not at all the enrobed, skull-capped man of the cloth I had imagined. We went into the hotel restaurant, all air conditioning, over-deferential staff and fruit-garnished buffet, although I had hoped to be swept off to some cathedral for a banquet or to a tortilla joint with salsa dancing and tequila. In fact it was very difficult to get anyone to take me anywhere, as people seemed to relish the opportunity to come into the Camino Real, use the pool and voice their loathing for it while jacking up my room service bill.

Michael Campbell Johnson was a notable exception to this rule and showed no interest in his surroundings as he sidled incongruously through them, apart from mentioning that he hadn't been here for years. We picked at a disgusting buffet lunch served too keenly by people who stared at me a lot and I asked him if I oughtn't to drink the water. Later, when I saw where and how he lives I was ashamed for asking. An over-cautious, non-Spanish-speaking idiot tourist in a posh hotel, despised by the locals, I imagined, for my ignorance and despised even more, I assumed, by the pseudo-locals like Eros and Tom.

Il Padre had been in El Salvador throughout the war. He seemed resigned to the horrors still going on today and shrugged at my suggestion that all this must surely shake his faith. 'There were some boys from our local *mara* (gang) who came in to play basketball yesterday at a time when they know they're not supposed to be there because the schools use the courts. I asked them what they were doing and they said hiding from the police – a nineteen-year-old boy had been killed up the road. I don't know if they were involved or not, but . . . Anyway, that was yesterday. Last week they found the body of a sixteen-year-old girl nearby . . . raped and murdered. You see?' I didn't.

He told me, chewing on a piece of fish, that he loved the country and the people. 'The ordinary people,' he qualified. I judged myself and decided I was wanting. I felt, in my white linen dress and with my fears about the water, that he might be putting me into the category of those who wouldn't understand the ordinary people of El Salvador whom he valued so much.

He got his address book out and started to recommend likely-sounding types for me to talk to about Dad in my quest to find out more about what happened than Scotland Yard had managed in their investigation the week after the event. 'I can't remember his name now,' he mumbled, staring at a spidery page. 'I have reached the second stage of growing old.' I raised my eyebrows. 'First you forget things, then you forget names, then you forget to do up your flies and then you forget to undo your flies in the first place.' I laughed, but despite the glare of the sun outside I was in a grim mood and felt a rush of pity for all these incontinent old men he referred to.

Like most westerners in El Salvador Father Campbell Johnson also remembered a time when the bar at the hotel was crowded with journalists and buzzing with morbid excitement, but he spoke of it wryly and without regret, as though their interest had been rather silly, if necessary to the cause. Or perhaps it was I who thought them silly, to be filing copy and drinking Scotch when there was real work being done by the likes of the priests and nuns who were hiding guerrillas, helping with medical supplies and comforting the bereaved – not interviewing and photographing them.

Eros, fiercely proud of his father's achievements, would disagree and say that the 'real journalists' were out there justifiably publicising atrocities even if there were some who just flew in and out and 'didn't know shit about shit'. I assumed my father was among the latter kind in his imagination, although dad did in fact know shit about Central America and loved it at least as passionately as Eros does.

Lying there by the pool where Dad had presumably lain, I could imagine him turning up at any moment – appearing through the glass doors with his tatty beige bag over his shoulder, squinting through his sunglasses and sweating into jeans and a blue shirt. The blue shirt which, some speculate, got him mistaken for a guerrilla and killed (though I do not now think this is likely).

Dad would have perched on the edge of the lounger, taken a swig of the nearest Coke and spat some complaints about what he had been doing that day. I curtailed this thought train since he would probably have thrown me into the pool, or made me dive for a silver dollar like he did when I was little (I still have it in my wallet). He hated me to be idle and was always teaching me to do something stupid (like play pool, eat oysters or stay underwater for a long time) or nagging me to write a diary.

I was rocking in a chair on the porch of the Red Lion Inn in Stockbridge Massachusetts (an olde worlde big American wooden deal with pretensions to antiquity – beautiful and now full of tourists, although then it was crumbling and creaking) looking at the stars and feeling lonely, when Dad threw a huge purple book into my lap. 'Why don't you write a diary?' he insisted, rummaging for a pen among bits of chewing gum, grains of tobacco and scraps of paper.

He was always anxious to keep me entertained, but he had usually brought a girlfriend along (perhaps to make it less stressful for both of us) so I was forever consigned to the back seat of some hire car, feeling sick and irritable, coughing in their smoke and not able to hear the conversation from the front. Also, if I didn't like whoever was occupying the passenger seat, I got told off.

'Don't read at dinner!' Dad said over lobsters in Cape Cod. 'Why not?' I asked, since I was allowed to read all the time when we were on our own – Dad always read the papers. This was a showdown and I won. I was reading through the complete works of P.G. Wodehouse and I certainly wasn't pausing to be asked whether I liked dolls or had a dog by someone who felt compelled to get on with me to save their relationship. I scowled and clung on to my book, always starting again at the beginning if I couldn't get back to the motel room to pick up the next one.

I catalogued all my grievances in the diary which Dad would try to find and read whenever he got the chance. My 1981 volume has 'Keep Off' smeared on its red leather front in pink glittery nail varnish.

Diary, 16 August 1981: today I watched TV while Dad went to the office. 86 degrees outside.

Diary, 17 August 1981: today I painted each nail a different colour with Evelyn's nail polish.

Unfortunately, I think he only got me to write a diary so that he could read it.

Diary, 24 August 1981: today I went to dad's office where I bought 16 postcards and wrote them after having a bath in the apartment. Had lunch with Louise Gubb and read the article on Harry's wedding that dad wrote in which my name was mentioned. Me and dad got a NY airline plane to Washington where we hired a car. Me and dad had a really good

laugh. We drove to the Jefferson hotel where dad
knows all the waiters who were lovely. We met
Shirley (Ugh! Yuck!). We had to sleep at her house.
Fuck! To bed.

Louise Gubb is a photographer and Harry is Harry Evans,
former editor of the *Sunday Times*, whose wedding on
Martha's Vineyard Dad and I had been to a week earlier.

Dad failed to keep off. I went down to breakfast at the
Jefferson a few days later and he rifled through my things
(he wasn't allowed in the dining room because it had a
dress code. He used to peek round the door and I would
throw muffins at him). He was cross with me and told
Shirley what I had written. (Ugh! Yuck! In fact she is now
a good friend of mine.) I vowed never to forgive him, but
I always did.

He took me to the Air and Space Museum in
Washington and bought me astronauts' freeze-dried ice-
cream. He took me to Rumplemeyer's ice-cream parlour
in New York for huge sundaes that made me feel sick. It
has a long zinc bar, pink walls, teddy bears and dolls everywhere and smiling waiters in white jackets with shiny buttons. We went for tea at the Plaza and asked the violinist
to play 'Teddy Bear's Picnic' (Dad's request not mine, but
I had to go up and ask). We went up the Empire State
Building, sailed round the Statue of Liberty and took
horse and carriage rides round Central Park. In the
evenings we went to cocktail bars where I would have
strawberry daiquiris without the daiquiri and Dad would
have gin martinis up with a twist. We ate oysters, threw
the cocktail biscuits at each other and laughed at people.

We always seemed to be staying in the most glamorous

hotels and I loved the glittering lifts, the lobby piano bars with twinkling lights in the dark ceiling, the black man in a white tux at the white baby grand and the sexy wait-resses carrying drinks with umbrellas in them.

Once when Dad was working I spent the whole day in the Boston Hyatt going up and down in the glass lifts that overlooked the fountains and plastic trees. Bernard was not afraid of heights. I made friends with the businessmen and old women who shared my lift and I bought water-melon-flavoured bubble gum at the news-stand.

I spent of lot of time alone in these hotels, reading end-lessly and waiting for Dad to come back from the bar. I slept badly and if we were sharing a room I was kept awake by him smoking and reading with the light on and then, once he had taking sleeping pills, snoring loudly. If we weren't sharing I would often be frightened or feel sick and think of excuses to go and wake him or (worse) them up.

Nowadays, alone in similar or sometimes the very same hotels I find myself still waiting up for him, sitting by the pool in great anticipation, exploring the bars and restau-rants as if looking for someone and watching the doors while I eat.

This time, in the Camino Real, the situation was acute and I would not have been remotely surprised to see him. 'What are you doing lolling around having Sammy Swimbles with these repulsive adolescents while I risk life and limb to keep you in the lap of luxury?' What am I doing? Trying to find out what happened to you, *actually*.

I persuaded Eros and his bedraggled friend Matt to accom-pany me to Sister Jean Ryan's house in a notoriously bad area of town not far from Mejicanos where my father was killed. I was afraid to out alone, which the boys found amusing, and since nobody was offering I had to virtually force people to escort me places. Embarrassing, but hey.

You can clearly see the deterioration in living conditions in San Salvador as you drive from area to area. Here there were lots of old colonial buildings visibly falling apart – no new businesses, no new buildings, lots of people out on the streets selling things and fewer private cars than elsewhere. We got a taxi from the hotel and Eros laughed with the driver, who had a crucifix hanging from his rearview mirror. He gave us religious leaflets when we got out ('Los pobres son los forjadores de nuestra historia – Monseñor Romero'). My limbs were sticking to the seat.

Sister Jean Ryan opened a wooden window in the middle of the door and peered through it. I felt as though we were trying to get into a speakeasy and ought to say 'Fingers Malone sent us', but her eyes smiled at us through the gap and she heaved the door open and let us into a cool, shady room around a tiny open courtyard containing a squat palm tree and big red flowers.

Jean Ryan has lived in El Salvador for more than twenty-five years, training novices and helping the poor. During the war many of her friends and colleagues were killed by government troops and she herself was routinely stopped and searched. Anyone religious was (often correctly) suspected of having links with the guerrillas. Now she works with prostitutes in downtown San Salvador as well as training the six novices who live with her. She admits that she doesn't know quite what she is doing with the prostitutes. 'I suppose I'm trying to show them that there is a spiritual side to life. To help them be better people,' she mutters, but says it is harder now to inspire people than ever it was during the worst atrocities of the war. 'They are just tired now,' she sighs, crossing her legs and smoothing her skirts. 'I had my watch taken off me the other day,' she laughed and sauntered off to the kitchen.

The boys and I exchanged smirks of complicity. When she came back she gave me some telephone numbers of people who might know which troops were stationed where in Mejicanos that day, 17 November 1989, when the FMLN staged their biggest offensive. She herself didn't remember the incident, she said, shaking her head. She brought a pot of tea in on a tray and she drank hers out of a cup with her Welsh dragon on it. We had slices of cake from a packet. Matt and Eros sipped their tea in bafflement and laughed. Afternoon tea with the British in San Salvador. 'Dude!'

We then took another taxi into an even poorer area up in the foothills of the volcano. Here there were very few buildings at all, only a lot of corrugated iron huts, dusty unpaved streets and thick green foliage. People were loafing around barefoot in groups and women were cooking out on the street. I felt sure a gang would pounce on us at any moment but Eros said, 'Just act like you're a real badass dude and they won't touch you.' I wasn't quite sure how to do this but he seemed to be carrying it off pretty effectively for all of us.

Michael Campbell Johnson had told us that he was based at the terminal of the 26 bus and that everyone would know it. Everybody kind of knew it but there were broken-down 26 buses all over the place and none of them looked likely. Eventually some raggy children pointed us towards a white wall with a bright mural all over it and a tall iron gate in it. Inside there was a court-yard and some low whitewashed buildings – one of them the room Michael Campbell Johnson lives in. It has bars on its one tiny window and is dark and crowded inside – a single bed, some teetering bookshelves and heaps of papers and boxes. There is an assembly room decorated with murals and memorabilia dedicated to Archbishop Romero, and the six Jesuit priests killed the day before my father. I had lain on an Atlanta porch drinking white wine in the sun and reading a book about their deaths that a nun, Pamela Hussey, had given to me in England. It was written by a close friend and associate of the dead priests, Father Jon Sobrino, and he described his feelings at hear-ing of the news of their deaths. Eventually, he resolved that good comes out of every evil. This made me cry and stamp my flip-flops on the porch. Maybe the deaths of the priests brought about change for the better, spurred peace-makers into action and left a legacy of goodness, but what about Dad? He didn't die for a cause. Nobody benefited. Most deaths do not bring about any positive change. They are everyday tragedies. No great matter – except for those left behind.

From behind the wall I could hear yelping. The parish dog and her puppies were playing on the steps. The little brown fluffy things were bounding idiotically about, slip-ping over their tails and biting each other's ankles. When one of them leapt up at its mother to feed she squealed – they had just grown teeth. She flattened her ears to her head and lowered it meekly, swinging her tail as her master approached.

He showed us the basketball courts at the back – dusty and grey but surrounded by palm trees. Members of the local gang were playing sullenly and others were sloping about by the concrete walls at the side. Two of them, Campbell Johnson suspects, were involved in the murder he had mentioned to me. Although all the kids were tattooed and moody looking, these boys were the most tattooed and most moody looking. They didn't play ball and they sulked quietly under a tree whispering to each other occasionally.

Eros, who has befriended and is photographing a different but equally deadly *mara* in San Salvador, took off his shirt, handed me his rucksack and grabbed a ball from some killer thug. Bad move, you might think, but he and Matt organised a two against two game and the sides were equally matched. After a few hoops had been shot the *mara* members loosened up and started laughing, muttering to each other and cheering their friends on. Eros fell through a grate and cut his leg quite badly but there was no question of stopping in humiliation as the blood seeped through his trousers. 'Yo, Brad!' Matt shouted as Eros aimed for the hoop. Local girls often ask if he is Brad Pitt. There are remarkable similarities, but I would be surprised if Brad was as good at basketball.

The *mara* members (who have similarly grim life expectancies to gang members in LA – they are all surprised to reach twenty-one) have graffitied the tarmac of the second basketball court with those Gothic gang letters you see on New York subway walls. Il Padre is proud of their artwork and hopes that through being able to come to him they might fall away from the *maras* and find a better life. Nobody is excluded from his munificence.

Dad would have liked it up here, I thought, watching two middle-class Californian boys shooting hoops with the *maras* in a Jesuit priest's back yard. Campbell Johnson put some antiseptic on Eros's wound and escorted us back through the darkening orange dust to the main volcano road where we got a hot petrol-smelling car with leopard-skin-nylon seat covers to take us down again. It was about half-past five when we passed the Camino Real on the way to Eros and Matt's house and as we approached it a huge cloud of green parrots flew over our heads towards the volcano where they sleep at night.

Walking up the steps on to his porch, Eros picked up the fallen mangoes from under the tree and batted the insects away from the porch light before he opened the door. The room was large, empty and dark with a low ceiling and a dim fluorescent strip light. Leafcutter ants carried bowls of fruit and large trees across the floor in an orderly line between a small kitchen table at one end of the room and a lurid orange plastic sofa at the other. The answering machine, unsurprisingly, had lots of messages from pleading girls on it – 'Ola! Eros!' – and they were smirkingly listened to while mangoes lazily lost their skins over a metal plate.

On the walls were violent photographs of gang fights and tattooed Latino thugs. 'My room mate has more money than me so he gets them printed up.' Room mate was not in evidence. Honduras apparently. Eros showed me his own photographs of Salvadorean girl gangs and their initiation rituals. He explained how a new recruit will be viciously kicked and beaten up for a pre-arranged period of time, say ten minutes, as part of her induction. There were pictures of a young girl in agony. Then a shot of the same girl being hugged and petted by her torturers while she clasped her stomach. 'They look after each other,' he said. He seemed impressed at their straight-forward brutality and kindness, the black and white view of the world. Why not skip the beating? I was wondering. The westerners I met out there had a odd fascination with the varying degrees of human cruelty and a seemingly endless amazement at its capacity to live alongside kindness.

I used to find the same thing in Russia. You would meet these violent gangsters and want them to be scarred and frightening, but really, in certain contexts, they were friendly and kind, husbands and fathers. Eros basically admired the gangs for their honest violence. 'They're straight-talking motherfuckers, man. "Hey! You wanna come to my place, man? I'll have my mamma cook for us, homey? When you comin' back man?" You know.' He seemed to imagine that I would take offence at this atti-tude. That I prefer a more 'civilised' society. 'Man,' he said, smiling without warmth. 'Civilised society thinks dropping bombs on Iraq is OK.'

I sat on the hideous sofa under the flickering greenish light and ate orange mango slices. Eros lamented the state of journalism which, he thought, had become too com-mercial, too provincial, less idealistic and increasingly meaningless. No arguing with that. I had been having dinner at Lemonia in Primrose Hill with some journalist friends just before I came and one of them, Rebecca Fowler of the *Mail on Sunday*, had been working at the *Sunday Times* as a trainee when my father was killed. It came up as a global message on everybody's computer and the whole office went quiet. 'I'd never seen anything like it and haven't since,' she said. The grief, she told me, had been enormous. People were crying and nobody knew what to do. 'It seemed to be the end not just of him, but of a whole era, the whole type of journalism that he embodied,' said Rebecca.

Eros, slurping mango juice carefully off his fingers first, handed me a faded but uncrumpled copy of *Rolling Stone* magazine. 'Look at the back page,' he said. He busied himself with something else. The back page was an obituary of his father – photographer, revolutionary, idealist. There he was, as beautiful as his son, sitting in a Salvadorean hammock. His murder, according to the piece, had been caught on film.

It was strange to be so reserved with someone, as Eros and I were with each other, someone who knew exactly what it was like. Someone who had had all their most trivial memories made overpoweringly important in the crack of a gunshot. Suddenly our lives could be condensed into before (nice) and after (horrible). When my dad died I put all my photos of him into an album. They all fitted neatly into one book that I could snap shut as though that somehow was that. Almost all my childhood memories of Dad would probably fit neatly into a chapter. 'Oh God,' I said, not specifically to Eros, imagining the footage and what it must have been like for the boy watching it. 'Yeah,' sighed Eros, looking away. 'That was some pretty sorry shit.'

Chapter Five

So runs my dream: but what am I?
An infant crying in the night:
An infant crying for the light:
And with no language but a cry.

1976–88

Dad quite often frightened me. He seemed to resent the fact that some people (like five-year-olds) weren't as afflicted with existential angst as he was, so he set about trying to rectify the situation. I had started sleepwalking and it terrified me. Mum caught me opening the front door once, I think, and I imagined that when I went to sleep I might wander out into the street and get completely lost, or never wake up and carry on for ever in the new life I had begun by just getting out of bed one night. I would creep from my room and never be seen again.

I was having tea at Kenwood House with Dad and I was eating some jelly trifle. It was hot and dogs chained up to the stair rails were lapping water out of empty ice-cream tubs. Dad was making jokes about my sleepwalking and I told him to shut up, not to talk about it, it was too frightening.

'Don't be silly,' he said. 'After all, you don't know whether that is more real than this. Maybe this is a dream and at night you wake up.'

Great. Thanks, Dad. I think it was after this conversation that my chronic and persistent insomnia set in. Ta very much.

But if he really wanted to send a chill down my spine, all he would have to say was 'Boggie Regis'. He might as well have been talking about the fiery pit of hell. I hated Boggie Regis. I hated going there and I hated talking about it. My grandfather Fred, Dad's dad, had retired to Littlehampton, near Bognor Regis, not long after I was born. When his wife, Nora, died in 1970 he married a lady called Millie, to whom the pregnant Nora Blundy had been evacuated during the war.

Grandpa and Millie lived in a yellow and white bunga-low on an old people's housing estate by a flat field with a horse in it. They had an eerily neat garden behind a tall white fence and a 'sun room' with yellow venetian blinds and a collection of horrible plates on little wire plate dis-player things on the walls. The plates had Chinese people with mad eyes on them, prehistoric looking birds and tangled patterns. There was a green velour footstool in the sitting room, lots of sinister little china ornaments of people carrying balloons, and a mustachioed staring emperor in a kimono that I would one day carry across the Atlantic in my lap. (I spilt some Bloody Mary on his head and was glad.) Millie always made creamed leeks. She laid the table with mats and condiments and superfluous cut-lery (table laying was not a thing with which I was at all familiar) and they had salt and pepper in aluminium insti-tutional shakers. Grandpa only used Imperial Leather soap and the whole place smelt of it. There were yellow nylon sheets and pink candlewick bedspreads in the guest bed-room. Dad and I slept there in twin beds – or at least Dad slept. I was kept awake by the snoring of father, from behind the wall, and son from the bed next to me. I could hear the sea.

There was tall, thin, cream furniture with gold patterns round the outside and swirly handles. It was too hot and too enclosed and too terrifying.

Grandpa had been ill since I could remember and he had trouble speaking because of a stroke. He dribbled and I couldn't tell what he was saying. He was amazingly tall and the sight of him hobbling along behind a Zimmer frame whose highest rung he could barely reach down low enough to grab hold of was chillingly awful.

Going down there upset Dad and he was always in an appalling mood on the way. If he didn't have a car we would hire one. He would get lost and stuck in traffic every single time we ever went and I would sit in the back and get sick. I usually managed to actually throw up, what with the cigarette smoke and angry driving, and this made him even crosser. He swore and spat.

If he happened to be taking a girlfriend he was easier to deal with because he would make a joke of how awful it was going to be and terrify her, thereby exorcising his own dread. If it was just me we would arrive with me pale-faced and pacing on the lawn and him thin lipped and smoking.

When Grandpa could still walk we would go down to the beach front and walk on the shingle in the wind and the cold, the grey sea roaring at us from behind its concrete breakers. A café there did stewed tea out of a huge urn, Wall's ice-cream and fat white buns with icing on top. I once had a strawberry milkshake in a tall sundae glass with a stripy straw and then spent the whole night throwing up bright pink liquid into the nylon sheets. I refused to be moved when sick. I haven't drunk a milk-shake since.

Grandpa was a Special Policeman during the war and he loved to talk about it. I didn't care, didn't know anything about the war and couldn't understand what he said anyway. I was so bored I wanted to scream. I found him disgusting, Millie fussing and irritable (I wasn't the kind of child she was used to) and I wanted to go home more than anything. Grandpa, of course, loved me and was bursting with pride for Dad. He had sent him to private school and seen him through university (Bristol) and now read his weekly pieces with disbelieving glee. He would have liked Mum and Dad to stay married (he forced Mum to address him as 'Dad') and would have preferred Dad not to bring German girlfriends to his house (Evelyn), but on the whole Dad was everything Grandpa had ever dreamed he might be.

I would love to hear his war stories now, walk along the beach with him and let him buy me a cup of tea and some ice-cream. I'd like to tell him how I was doing at school and paint him a picture to stick up on the fridge. Sorry, Grandpa.

When Millie, who was dying of cancer, couldn't look after him any more, he was moved into a nursing home and Mum and I would go down to visit him there. He flirted with the nurses and sat looking out to the garden that led down to the sea. I roller-skated. Dad sent him American election campaign memorabilia that he showed off to us.

Dad, unsurprisingly, was stricken with guilt and was unable to bear the idea of his father in a home. He made me promise never to put him in one when he got old. I said he'd be lucky if I found one for him anything like as nice as Grandpa's. I swore I would never visit him.

Obituary by Andrew Stephen, the 'Observer', 18 November 1989
There was also a hint of sadness, even loneliness, in the very gregariousness that made him so popular. Many women loved him, but the two unchanging constants in his life were his daughters Anna and Charlotte.

It was impossible to imagine him growing old. It is a cliché to say so, but no less true for that: we all loved him, and the world is the poorer this weekend without his presence.

From Middleton-on-Sea, Littlehampton, near Bognor Regis I think Dad got his fear of English mediocrity, tea houses, families, old age, ordinary suburban life. It was infectious. The very sight of a display cabinet for ornaments or a wipe-clean surface makes me want to get into my car and drive very fast as far as possible.

Washington, DC, circa 1975
Dear Anna,

Grandpa from Boggie Regis (ho ho! you can't clump me!) is coming to America next week to see Pauline [Dad's sister]. I wish I had my mac – it's raining. Children started going to school here this week. They go in buses with police cars, police motorcycles, policemen. Mummy will tell you why unless she is too silly to know.

Love, Daddy

Washington, DC, 1988

The most irritating phrase I have heard recently is 'complimentary beverage' which they keep saying on the Pan Am shuttle. It makes my flesh creep. It affects me in the same way that 'Boggie Regis' used to make your blood boil, that is when you weren't vomiting out of the car window.

We eventually solved the Bognor Regis = Misery problem by discovering Bailiffscourt Hotel in nearby Climping. Bailiffscourt is heaven. Log fires, low-beamed ceilings, creaking doors, dark panelling, four-poster beds, secret passageways, tea on the lawn, sandy beaches, banks of daffodils and glades of bluebells, a swimming pool in summer and horses in the yard waiting for me to ride them.

It cost a fortune but Dad didn't care. Anything not to have to sleep between the nylon sheets and smell the sickness. Dad brought a girlfriend (they loved it) and I was usually allowed to bring a friend. My little friend Karl Reynolds (named after Karl Marx) broke the sink in the ladies' loos by sitting on it to talk to me. We crept down secret passages, had midnight feasts of food we had collected from meals during the day and Karl fell off his horse. The whole escapade was completely transformed.

Now Boggie Regis was a treat rather than a chore and I would plead to be allowed to go down there and ride horses along the beach.

When Grandpa died in 1977 Dad was on a plane with President Reagan asking him whether he thought Dad should go back and be with his sick father. The President thought he should. Dad rushed back on Concorde at the last minute but he didn't make it. I stayed in a depressing hotel in Arundel (mini-bar, trouser press) during the funeral which I wasn't allowed to attend.

Millie died soon afterwards. She actually died while Mum and I were in the hospital. I remember seeing her – bald, spoon fed, lying there. Ghastly.

After Dad was killed I went back to Middleton-on-Sea, to Bailiffscourt on the first of my many pilgrimages. My first attempt to find Dad and get a measure of him. I stood outside the yellow and white bungalow wondering at its drabness, wondering where they'd all gone – the impossibly tall old man, and round woman in the nylon dress, the young man with the cigarettes and the car keys (escape!) and the little girl in the stripy swimming costume.

I ate tea on the lawn at Bailiffscourt and watched some children making a daisy chain. I walked along the beach and saw people riding horses in the surf. I could see what it was Dad had been terrified of and I could see what it was he was trying to create instead. Well, he succeeded. No nursing home, no suburbia, no radiotherapy, no bottles of multi-coloured pills by his dinner plate and no reluctant visits from churlish grandchildren.

And was it worth it? Was he glad when they wheeled him into the Rosales that he wasn't in a British seaside hospital with me and my sister Charlotte and our children at his bedside saying all the things we wished we'd said before? Probably he was.

Letter of condolence from Wendy Ormond, November 1989
Dearest Anna,

You do not know me. I met your father just three weeks ago in Washington DC . . . No matter what happens to you in life – no matter where you are – you should always feel proud to be David Blundy's daughter. When Charlotte is old enough to understand, I hope you will tell the same to her.

Going to Bailiffscourt was equal only, in terms of picturesqueness and glamour, to going to Robert Harling's house. I always associated being with Dad with entering another world of lovely things and beautiful people, and the Harlings' house seemed to me the perfection of everything to which I aspired as I sat reading Jane Austen books in Crouch End.

They live behind creaking iron gates, up a worn gravel path between tall, dark pine trees. The house itself is a pinkish terracotta with white patches where the stone has crumbled away and battlements at the top. There are faceless lions guarding the front gate and ivy creeping over the window frames. Daffodils surround it in spring and a landscape of bleak trees stretches before it in winter.

Inside, dusty chandeliers hang from the ceiling and ancient busts stand austere on the black and white marble flagging of the hall. It was like a princess's house, where you could sweep down a staircase in your ballgown, have a maid bring you tea in a silver pot by the log fire, or wait for your lover in a silk négligé and a four-poster bed.

Robert and Phoebe Harling, probably in their sixties when I first met them, were devastatingly glamorous. Robert, then editor of *House and Garden*, was brash and forthright and wore jodhpurs and boots. Phoebe was delicate and beautiful, bright white hair arranged high on her head, her long slim legs in stockings and her ears, wrists and fingers decorated with intricate jewellery. They had maids who pushed food through a hatch into the dark dining room, a room dominated by a dusty turquoise and green chandelier, a dark round table and paintings of different types of apples on the walls. Sedate as the atmosphere always seemed to be, it was inevitably shattered by Robert's conversational gambits. Robert loves to talk about sex. He can't help telling women they look 'delicious' (if they do – I am always insulted these days when he doesn't say it) and he developed a knack for embarrassing me (and probably everybody else) horribly. In my early teens, when sex was almost all I ever thought about, I felt he was reading my mind and was speechless with humiliation. All he actually said was something like, 'Must be about ready for boyfriends now, Anna?' but Dad would flinch towards his cigarettes and I would cringe.

Once, on my seventeenth birthday, I had a joint dinner party in an Indian restaurant in Finchley called Bengal Bertie's with my friend Dan Levy. I drank seventeen glasses of white wine and then we went back to Dan's house where somebody handed me a fat joint. I was sitting on the stairs smoking when I suddenly stopped having any awareness of what was up and what was down. I toppled into the front garden and lay in the grass, throwing up. My boyfriend at the time was a Goth called Simon who had long black hair, a black cape and who smelt of patchouli oil. He came to sit with me and he laid my head in his lap while I was sick. Every time he leant over me the smell of his perfume made me throw up again. I wanted to tell him to go away but I couldn't speak. 'God, she looks dead!' someone squealed as they walked past me.

Obviously, neither of my own parents could feasibly be called, so my friend Clare had her dad come from Potters

Bar to pick us up in his red BMW. I had told her to get an ambulance but she judged wisely (she always does).

Insanely resilient as people are at that age, I woke up in Clare's lovely low-beamed house feeling fine, if a tiny bit delicate. Dad, baffled at my appearance somewhere so far from home (we had thought up some totally unconvincing excuse for why I had come back to Clare's), came to get me for lunch at Robert and Phoebe's.

Dad and I were always a rigid hour and a half late. We always hit traffic in Tooting. We always bought Phoebe flowers from the same shop and they had always wilted by the time we got there. I was always carsick (but less so than on the way to Bognor Regis).

Phoebe was glittering and elegant and I felt ridiculous in my black party clothes from the night before. I looked macabre in a long Cruella De Vil dress, silver chain belt and heavy eye-liner. I was, however, starving. Robert asked how my party had been and did I have a boyfriend and were we having sex yet. I blushed and mumbled and stared at my roast pork. 'Jesus Christ,' rasped Dad and Robert laughed. He then started talking about orgies, and how it would do a man the power of good to see his wife made love to by another man. I failed to see how this could be good for anyone's self-confidence but piped down because maybe, I reasoned, one was only sexually unselfconfident as a teenager. Little did I know that was about as uninhibited as I was ever likely to get.

Dad told a long and funny story, rocking backwards and forwards in his chair, about how ludicrous Christian Scientists were and how he had done a story about some of these half-witted lunatics who were letting their child die of appendicitis or something. 'It was just so fucking idiotic,' he concluded. 'Nobody here's a Christian Scientist, are they?' he asked, smirking.

'Well, I was actually raised in Christian Science,' announced a formerly silent American woman whom nobody had much noticed before. While the rest of us concentrated on our food and sniggered, Dad spent half an hour trying to wheedle out of his hour-long, vitriolic *faux pas*. The woman didn't mind at all – she was all blushes and smiles and was clearly relieved to have come up with a way of making him pay attention to her. I'm sure she would be one of the women whom I still find myself sitting next to at dinners all over the world who get watery-eyed and red-faced when I tell them my name.

The last time I went to see the Harlings with Dad we took Charlotte with us. It seemed at the time to be a defining visit. Me as adult, Dad with new daughter, things settling down for the better. It was summer 1989 and I had been given a sapphire and diamond ring by my boyfriend, Giles, and I was calm and superior as a result – somebody loves me I don't need you any more, type of thing. Charlotte was about one year old, gurgly and smiling. Dad was just elated to be with her. We ate lunch outside at the back of the house, Robert with a blue bandanna round his straw hat, matching the turquoise of his eyes. Tess, my border collie, bounded about the grounds, overheating in the sun.

Yes I had a boyfriend, yes I had sex with him, yes I loved him, were my answers this time. Dad could wince as much as he liked. Charlotte lay down on a sun lounger and fell asleep on her back, giggling while Dad tickled her tummy. The snail was in his shell and all was right with the world.

He was killed later that year.

I have been to the Harlings' three or four times since, dragging stray boyfriends, trying to make it all the same again. Last summer I was just about to fly off to Sardinia at a moment's notice to join a man who said he loved me but who wouldn't sleep with me.

'That doesn't sound any good, Anna,' snarled Robert derisively. I wasn't listening, which was stupid and arrogant considering his vastly greater experience. He was right. It wasn't any good in the long run, although the Sardinia bit was lovely. 'I'm not interested in how you get there any more, Anna,' Robert said. 'I'm only interested in the final result.' Don't come here without a husband again.

One of the things that always made being with Dad seem so dream-like and wonderful was that we were constantly going to places that I only knew about from films or songs. Most grandiose, of course, were all the biblical places. It could only have been with Dad that I went to Bethlehem for lunch with a Palestinian family ('Oh little town . . .') or swimming in a back garden pond in Jericho ('Joshua fought the battle of . . .'). Never mind Jerusalem. Well, these feet did.

In New York we ate in the red leather seats of the Russian Tea Rooms (*Tootsie*), watched New York light up from the Rainbow Room in the Rockefella Plaza (*Sleepless in Seattle*, among others), sat watching the rowers from the Boathouse in Central Park (*When Harry Met Sally*) and ate oysters at Elaine's (Woody Allen films and Billy Joel songs). Dad knew Elaine (you had to know Elaine) and it was a supposed honour if she sat down at your table for a drink. She sat down at our table for a drink and I was deeply unimpressed. I was about eleven. She seemed to me to be fat and loud. Now of course I am incredibly impressed that I know Elaine and I shall milk it for all it's worth if I ever go there again, which is unlikely because I've forgotten where it is.

New York, 1989
Had dinner with ben in elaine's (she doesn't remember you). wore a dinner jacket and went with jodi cobb to the centennial of national geographic at the sheraton. Bush made one of the worst speeches I have ever heard. It was deadly boring except for the speeches by edmund hillary, mary leakey and that woman who studies apes in tanzania, whatsername goodall. they were very moving, but my throat felt tight under the bow tie so I left and went down the guards for a double gin martini with Kev.

Anyway, I don't care if she remembers me or not. I was sick after those oysters, although that could have been the colossal ice-cream sundae I ate in Serendipity afterwards.

And it wasn't just the places, of course, it was the people too.

'Oh fuck,' said Dad, pacing the room, Chrysler Building sparkling in the blue behind him. 'This weekend?' he dragged the phone lead behind him and made find-me-a-cigarette faces at me, picked up sheets of paper and shook crumpled, empty packets in vain. I went next door and found a pack in the bedroom. I hid it behind some books.

He poured the rest of the strong, cold coffee out of the

jug in the dark galley kitchen where cockroaches lurked and into his half-empty cup, hunching the receiver between shoulder and ear and trailing the laces of his trainers. 'I could fly down with Holden,' he said and raised a did-you-find-any? eyebrow at me. I shook my head and pottered off into the bathroom to do my nails.

Dad rapped a fingernail on the door and rattled the handle. 'Let me in!' he whined, kicking it open. 'Do you want to be a bridesmaid?' he asked, ruffling my hair. 'Get *off*!' I said, scowling.

I did want to be a bridesmaid. Harry Evans was marrying Tina Brown at Ben Bradlee's house in East Hampton and we were going. I was really excited. I had brought my white and pink stripy dress across the Atlantic in case of just such an eventuality.

We flew out of La Guardia on some ridiculously small thing with two seats and a couple of slapped-together propellers. La Guardia is, or was, incredibly old-fashioned altogether, really uninspiring confidence-wise. It's just an aircraft hangar basically, without any noticeable air traffic control or mechanics or anything. Dad had a hotdog and said it was the most evil tasting little fucker he had ever encountered. We laughed a lot and he said he felt sick.

Dad and Tony Holden, whom we met at the airport, had chartered the plane at great expense to take us to Long Island. They might have been drunk, but they were certainly very excited about the venture and they kept having to move about in the back after take-off because they were upsetting the balance. There was no room for me so I sat up front with the pilot in the co-pilot's seat. No co-pilot. Probably died in last week's crash. I was reading the Jeeves and Wooster story about the cow creamer that

Bertie somehow has to steal or retrieve from his aunt. Dad kept telling me to keep my eyes on the view (sea, islands). 'Look out the window, you ungrateful little creep. What kind of a daughter are you?' 'Alleged daughter,' I corrected him. The pilot looked at me nervously. We landed (amazingly) and crawled out into the sunlight over the wing, all relieved to be alive. I was in my full wedding regalia (pink and white deal) but Dad and, I think, Tony, were in jeans.

Ben Bradlee's house is where Jackie O grew up and it looks that way. A big white American wooden thing with porches and eaves. I loved it. I felt it only fitting that I should have chartered a plane to come here and should then be served lemonade on the porch with newspaper owners, writers and editors – Mort Zuckermann who coptered into the garden, and Nora Ephron, who lent me her swimming costume. Bradlee was a grand old patriarch who sat in his wicker chair with the air of a man whose newspaper had brought down a government with the most famous scoop in history. I wonder if he was like this before Watergate. This is you want your pilot, surgeon, ship's captain, president to look like if you have a choice. Nothing will go wrong with this guy at the helm.

Tina, a old friend of Dad's, was picking her bouquet in the garden and I went to help her. She confided in me things I didn't understand and that I wish I could remember about the nature of marriage and how she felt. I just remember her whispering urgently and happily to me, and my understanding that this was extremely important in some way.

It was hot and there were white paper bells adorning the platform where they would say their vows. Harry had disappeared somewhere in the car and the time was drawing nigh. Dad idiotically pretended to be worried and managed to infect everyone else. Where-the-fuck-is-hes ricocheted off the porch furniture.

There was a man there who was introduced to me as Hatpin and who looked exactly as I imagined P.G. Wodehouse's Gussie Finknottle to look. I liked him immediately. The judge who was to perform the ceremony turned up in a shiny suit and reflector shades.

Harry, of course, arrived on time and Bradlee played the wedding march on a crackling tape recorder that he had hidden behind a bush. Afterwards I sprayed JUST MARRIED on the blue hire car in shaving foam and everyone got drunk by the pool. Dad was getting a kick out of my meeting and being unimpressed by all these eminent people. It wasn't that I was blasé, I genuinely hadn't heard of them. I have now, and I am stunned to have spent such a casual day with them. When I meet Ben Bradlee nowadays I put on a suit and summon up my best anecdotes.

Hatpin was at my Dad's memorial service and he introduced himself to me as John Heilpern, diffidently, as though I might not know him. He laughed when I shouted 'Hatpin!' and kissed him. You don't forget a name like that.

'Good Times, Bad Times' by Harold Evans
I was due on holiday in America. While there, I had the pleasure of reading in the *Times* court page that Tina Brown and I were married on 19 August at Grey Gardens, East Hampton, Long Island, the beautiful summer home of the editor of the *Washington Post*, Ben Bradlee, and his wife, the writer Sally Quinn.

With Tina's parents in Spain, the bride was given
away by Tony Holden, who had taken a house on
Martha's Vineyard with Amanda and his children.
The *Sunday Times* foreign correspondent David
Blundy, who had just returned from El Salvador, and
his daughter, Anna, came in from Manhattan, as did
John Heilpern, the *Times* arts correspondent in the
United States and his wife Joan Buck, the writer. The
other guests were the novelist Nora Ephron and
Mortimer Zuckermann, the publisher of *Atlantic*. The
ceremony took place in the Bradlees' Italian garden,
on the edge of the Atlantic, with Ben as the best man
and young Anna Blundy as the maid of honour.

Diary, 20 August, 1981: We bought carnations and
went to Ben Bradlee's house which is huge. It has a
pool. Harry Evans, 53, married Tina Brown, 27 (!) in
the garden. They both cried. I was bridesmaid. It was
lovely.

From there we flew to Martha's Vineyard in our plane, to
join Tony Holden and his wife, Amanda, and their sons in
the house they had rented for the summer. It was creaking and wooden and by the sea. We had a picnic on
William Styron's private beach (someone summarised
what they thought might be the plot of *Sophie's Choice* to
me and I somehow got the impression that Styron himself
had been in a concentration camp – I remember feeling
desperately sorry for him, despite his $1,000 a square foot
beach) and we were taken via motor-powered dinghy,
aboard a huge wooden and brass yacht with sails and a
crew. Dad made me jump off it into the sea at

Chappaquiddick amid lots of jokes I didn't get for another decade or so. It was a long way down. Dad dived in, flailingly. Tony Holden's son, Sam, asked his dad to leave him his brown shoes when he died. Tony said he would.

One night I played poker with Dad and Tony: they got very drunk so I won. It was dark and I think we were playing by candlelight. They drank whisky and I could hear the sea as I concentrated very hard on the rules.

Diary, 21 August 1981: The boat where we had clam chowder was called 'Nor Easter'. I won $6 off Dad and Tony. I called Dad a jerk and chucked Tony's money in his wine. Everyone laughed.

Letter of condolence from Tony Holden
Do you remember vacations on Martha's Vineyard?

I don't want to intrude on your own memories or your feelings, but I wanted to tell you that David was a great deal more than the whacky, wayward, listless soul so widely depicted. He was a guy of fierce honesty in his work and his dealings with people; of lucid intelligence, impatient with hypocrisy and self seeking; of great moral courage, discarding rank and status in his search for the truth in things, public and private; of relentless determination to prick pomposity, expose evasiveness and cut through the crap between him and the clues to what the hell this life is all about.

A gypsy, sure, a wandering minstrel, but a man who enriched the lives of others perhaps at the expense of his own. He made me a better journalist, a better person, able to make better use of my time and my inclinations, simply by being around him. Ten years of Dave enabled me to make much more of the rest of my life.

I found photos from Harry's wedding when I was sorting through Dad's stuff for this book. I don't remember having seen them before, and there is one of Dad sitting at a round table on the porch with his sleeves rolled up talking to people. Photos I'm not used to always send him leaping out at me, alive as ever, saying something ludicrous. The curve of his back and the gesture of his forearms is so achingly familiar. I want to go up and hang round his neck. 'Off, you little bleeder!' he would say, laughing. 'Anna, this is Mort, Sally, Nora. This is my alleged daughter, Anna Catherine Blundy.'

Things like Harry's wedding we could do together and both have a good time.

But there were certain tasks Dad was forced to perform out of sheer altruism.

Dad hated Disneyland. He hated the queues. He hated the overweight Americans. He hated the cutesyness. He hated the tack. The very thought of some themed hotel with Mickey Mouse soap and a monorail direct to the park sent shivers down his spine. He sighed and growled and smoked and drank and paced backwards and forwards like one of the wolves in London Zoo that you can see from Regent's Park. He was there for my sake and he made that absolutely clear.

We had been to journalist John Barnes's house near Malibu Beach and had swum in the sea. We went to Universal Studios and got snapped at by the shark that played Jaws in the film. I had had my picture taken on the Walk of Fame in my yellow teapot dress and had drunk daiquiris without the daiquiri at the Beverly Hills Hotel.

All I needed now was to go to Disneyland. As far as I was concerned it was magical. To see Cinderella's castle lit up by fireworks and to be surrounded by so much pink – my dream world. I was elated to see the Disney characters live and waddling about the place in the appalling heat, but my elation was slightly muted by Dad's derision. He skulked there, hunched and nicotine clouded, by the entrance to Pirates of the Caribbean while I went to see Pluto close up.

Then he forced me to queue up for Space Mountain and I cried for half an hour in terror. Dad said it was too late to turn back once we had started queuing. When we got to the bit where you had to be fastened in there was a sign telling people with heart trouble that they shouldn't ride. Immediately Dad was stricken with clammy terror and was insisting on being allowed out of the enclosure. 'Are you displaying symptoms of heart trouble, sir?' asked an attendant, slightly confused by such worries on the part of a clearly robust, tanned, muscular, tall thirty-five-year-old. 'Well, not as such,' mumbled Dad as they hustled us in. I loved it. He hated it. 'Oh Christ. Oh God,' he whispered as we careered round in the dark.

He liked the haunted house best. I sort of liked it, but was genuinely terrified in the lift as the walls grow longer and the room closes in. We both loved the graveyard with the skeletons rising from their coffins. Dad grabbed my shoulder and shook it spectrally. 'Grip of death,' he mumbled. He did this quite a lot outside of the haunted house ride as well.

My favourite ride though, was It's A Small World. Cute. Dolls. Baby pinkness. Fluffy nationalism. There is nothing frightening about It's A Small World (at least in the direct physical sense) and I insisted on going on it about a hundred times both in Disneyland and, one summer later, in Disneyworld, Florida where I saw an armadillo by the hotel pool and forked lightning from the balcony in a tropical storm. Dad was nauseated and fuming.

It would not be possible to say that he watched patiently in the evenings when I demanded to go to the themed hotel dinners. There was a magician there who was obliged to involve the children in his show. They always picked me, probably because they felt sorry for me, alone with a grumpy-looking man who might, or might not as far as they were concerned, have been my father.

It was only a few years later that people began to assume I was his girlfriend. Dad and his girlfriend Samira held a party in their flat in Tufnell Park when I was in my mid-teens and a friend of Sam's went rushing up to her to say: 'Dave's getting very friendly with that woman over there.'

I was irritated that he was so moody in Disneyland, and wondered later why he couldn't have pretended to he having a good time for my sake. I mean, how bad could it be? At least, I wondered these things until I took my own little sisters, Charlotte, and Mum's daughter, Grace, to Disneyland Paris in 1996. Here the tophatted doormen of the haunted house shouts 'A Jamais!' to the guests as they close the door on your doom.

I stood glowering in the interminable queues, had my hand over my mouth in It's A Small World, gripped the carriage in terror on the rollercoasters, got irritated when the girls wouldn't eat the revolting and expensive food on offer, refused to buy them the trinkets they wanted until they completely wore me down, and spent the whole time at Buffalo Bill's Wild West Show having a panic attack and hyperventilating.

Oh, *this* is what it's like taking people to Disneyland, I thought. I apologise, Dad, for judging you so harshly. Now I realise how mild-mannered, gentle and patient you were throughout the whole experience. A model of self-discipline and reserve, achieving heights of duplicity that I can only marvel at.

'It's a small world, after all. It's a small world after all. Though the rivers are wide and the mountains are tall, it's a small world after all.' Enough to drive anyone insane.

It was these kinds of nightmare parental tasks, that nobody likes doing but everybody has to, that I never associate with Dad. I can only think of him as someone as unfatherly as it is possible to imagine. But actually, in mulling over his role in my life, I realise that he did do a lot of things I had always deemed him incapable of.

The school porter poked his head round the door into the rows of maroon-clad girls, slumped over their desks, peering through their greasy fringes up at the yellow-chalked board. The Barbican Centre, which by 1984 had already begun to look grotty, stood grimly outside the windows on the other side of the fountains. This stretch of water was a prison moat as far as the inmates were concerned. From our sweaty, blue-lino classrooms we could see people lunching in the sun, couples kissing, schoolboys slouching, children eating ice-cream.

'Anna Blundy?' asked the porter.

I looked up from carving 'I love Boy George' into the desk with the twisted nib of my ink pen (one of those transparent ones with little hearts on it that you had to have).

'There's a man outside says he's your father. Do you want to come and tell me if you recognise him?'

I laughed. I already knew it was him. This was the man who always bleeped on the airport metal detectors and whom customs officials routinely stopped. 'If we could just take a look in those bags, sir?' You could almost see the grenades under his leather jacket, he looked so much like a terrorist. If you were a terrorist organisation this was the last man you'd choose to blow up the plane. Too obvious. Too conspicuous.

For the first time in his life he was half an hour early. He had also gone to the wrong gate – the front gate where they had someone to check for paedophiles. The experts congregated round the back where we actually came out. I went downstairs with the porter to positively identify the guy in the jeans, trainers and leather jacket, loping up and down with a hunch, smoking and glancing suspiciously up at the building through his reflector shades. He was unshaven and had brought the dog, who was going to have to sit in the car while I, Dad and my friend Lucy went to tea at the Waldorf.

Usually when Dad said he would meet me out of school he turned up hours late, leaving me standing alone in a playground. Occasionally he wouldn't turn up at all. At every carol concert or school play I was ever in I spent most of the performance leaning out of the wings to see if he had come, and he was so tall that I could always spot him straightaway. The trouble was, as far as trying to allay the heartsinking feelings and tears was concerned, he sometimes came even when he said he wasn't going to, so I could never just stop hoping and I could never crush down the disappointment when he didn't show. The same went for birthday phone calls.

Diary, 11 April 1982: My birthday! Dad didn't call from Baghdad. I am really really worried.

On the other hand, I did occasionally get compensatory birthday telegrams.

11 April 1984
The price on the sony walkman is not as obvious as it should be but if you look carefully you will see that it is 47 jordanian dinars. at the rate of exchange, that is buying dinars for dollars, that is approximately (given three dollars to the dinar) 3 X 47 = 141. As the pound has now dropped on the exchange markets against the dollar we can take the wall street selling rate for dollar against the pound, and that is roughly 1.35 dollars to the pound. So the cost of the Sony Walkman in pounds sterling is 141 + 1.35 = 104. 44444444444444 (pounds sterling). I thought you ought to know that. Happy Fourteenth birthday love daddy.

I left a City of London carol concert that year snivelling pathetically to myself because Dad's face hadn't loomed idiotically out of the crowd and I started wandering off to Moorgate tube on my own. Suddenly he appeared out of the gloom chasing after me in an ill-fitting suit, saying he'd been late and they wouldn't let him in, but he'd heard my solo anyway from outside . . . I think he was lying but I didn't care.

In 1981 he flew in from New York to see me play Oliver in the Campsbourne Junior School production in Crouch End. My boyfriend, Darren, was the Artful Dodger and I still have a photo of us, arm in arm, glowing and singing 'Consider Yourself'. We performed it in the assembly hall that smelt of parquet polish and had badly drawn pictures of Henry VIII on the walls. I swore to Mum and Dad that I would marry Darren Verschoor and they laughed and assured me I'd change my mind. Mum occasionally reminds me of it now. I must look him up.

Diary, Wednesday, 8 April 1981: the best ever night of my life. Oliver! Mum, Ricky and Dad were at the party afterwards.

I always had three parents at school events instead of the obligatory pair, and sometimes I managed to rustle up a fourth. I was appalled when Dad brought his girlfriend Shirley to a City of London open day. She went round the dining room to each of my teachers, in front of whom parents were expected to queue, and listened attentively to news of how I was doing in all my subjects (averagely). They had to pull up two extra chairs for my little collection and I was incredibly embarrassed. Even more than the girl whose mum looked like Diana Dors – she had come in a white mink coat with her bleached back-combed hair sculpted on to a lavishly made-up head. The occasion must, I see now, have been far worse for Shirley than for me. I will never, ever go out with anyone who has adolescent daughters from a previous relationship.

By the time I entered Westminster in 1986, Dad had already started to mature into something resembling a father. It was deeply disconcerting. Nobody tried to arrest him as he approached the school and people even seemed to assume that he might have some genuine business there. He managed to come and meet my housemaster in a suit and, arriving with Mum and Ricky, they were not the only troika of parents. By this age quite a few marriages had failed.

Dad asked the prospective housemaster, TJP, if Westminster had a drugs problem and (although the boys lolling darkly in the yard outside said, 'No, we've got plenty!') he answered honestly. Dad was sagely impressed. Whenever they found anyone in possession of drugs they expelled them immediately, he said. That was the most they could do. Dad didn't quip or laugh or wink at me. He seemed genuinely concerned about the issues surrounding my education (unsurprising considering the crippling cost – this whole escapade was at my own insistence) and he nodded, coughed and looked as though he wanted a cigarette. So did TJP, I shouldn't wonder.

At the sherry evening just before the start of term in 1986, Dad put his suit on again to stand in a corridor and smoke with the other hard-drinking, chain-smoking divorcee whose daughter would be in Busby's, my house. Dad's new friend mistook my mum for the offspring who would be incurring the vast expense. I had already singled out my prey for the Westminster years (actually I think Mum pointed him out to me) – the head of my house in a denim jacket and jeans and looking sultry in the corner. I smiled. He didn't blush. It was going to be a tricky one.

It was at this stage that Dad suddenly started showing more than passing interest in my education. I think he was impressed by the cobblestones and cricket whites of Westminster and he was staggered when I got into Oxford. His sneaking jealousy showed in his derisive letters.

Washington DC, 1988
Why have you dropped French (why not?) and why are you only doing three years instead of four. why are you doing that slavic thing. why do you keep sliming off at the weekends. I enjoyed my three years at all souls immensely, those languid dinners at the top table, the fine claret, the erudite conversation about the early tribal origins of the Gadafa, the long discussions about etruscan art. Ah, how the memories flood back. I remember old nikko stinkwinkle and our chats in ancient greek as we ambled by the banks of the vast river that rippled past the front door of my palatial suite in the ancient hall i lived in. Oh those games of billiards in the rat and ferret. sorry to hear you have already run out of money, but the chill bite of the wind will take your mind off the nagging hunger and the rickets. talking of cricket i do hope you have continued the great blundy tradition in the nets. Ah, how the memories flood back, those halcyon days batting merrily on the banks of the river ooze. the problem with letters is that you can't just put the phone down if it gets boring. you have to hammer away to the end.

Now of course I am glad he did hammer away to the end

of these letters – I can exactly imagine his voice saying them, and they still make me laugh as much now as they did at the time.

Ian Jack (editor of 'Granta'), the 'Independent', November 1989
No one has ever made me laugh as much as David Blundy, and now I don't suppose anyone ever will.

Chapter Six

And I should tell him all my pain,
And how my life had droop'd of late,
And he should sorrow o'er my state
And marvel what possess'd my brain;

May 1997

'Well, they all seem a bit left wing,' someone mumbled into the receiver as I rapped my fingernails against a glass table top in Atlanta. This woman had lived in El Salvador during the war and at some stage she had adopted a baby there. I read her my list of contacts, scrabbled together in London over lunches with journalists and nuns.

'Are they?' I asked, not quite sure what she meant. Not enough death squad leaders? No murderers at all?

Well, I reasoned, better get as balanced a picture as possible, and I wrote down some of the names and numbers she was rattling off. Lots of wives of former presidents ('But wasn't he the one who . . ?') and other glitzy-sounding types who had been forced to entertain whatever foreign dignitaries had dared to come over in those days. Now they were obviously rotting away in their villas keen to talk to anyone who would still talk to them. (Me.)

The volcano had gone black and I was fiddling with the special butterfly-wrapped Camino Real chocolate that the staff had so kindly placed on my pillow that evening and was hoping I wouldn't have to sit in alone watching *Look*

Who's Talking Too dubbed into Spanish. I decided to take matters into my own hands and call a guy whom the lady in Atlanta had claimed was her closest friend in Salvador.

I said my clever bit of Spanish ('Buenas tardes') to his maid and he came to the phone immediately, seeming almost unreasonably keen to see me despite having just leapt off a flight from Los Angeles. 'What are jew doing right now?' he asked. 'I'll see jew een the lobby after twenty minutes.' I told him I had long blonde hair and would be wearing a green silk dress.

I was quite looking forward to meeting him, as it happened, because I figured that if he was right wing he would be rich and able to take me to some of the bars and clubs that Tom and Eros wouldn't go to. Those, that is, reserved for one per cent of the population. I wanted to dance salsa and drink tequila and not talk about the war.

I went downstairs at the appointed time, anticipating the lavish dinner and lakes of mescal I would be treated to by my glamorous new friend.

There in the lobby was a fat old man with a T-shirt stretched over his paunch, thick coiffed grey hair swept back off his face and a set of super-butch car keys hanging from his fingers. He stared at me from the depths of a beige sofa for a few seconds before realising that I was the person he had come to meet.

'Mees Blandy! Ay deeeen reyallize jew was so jong!' he explained.

'I just turned twenty-seven,' I said. 'But I feel about 127.'

I wanted to tell him that I hadn't realised he would be so old, but thought it might seem churlish. Anyway, comforting to go off for a nice avuncular drink, I thought. Just because he's right wing doesn't have to mean he's a mass-murdering lunatic, I tried to explain to myself.

The trouble is, I knew that was exactly what it probably did mean, and you can tell soon as look at these types that they are compromised beyond the boundaries of humanity. Even before he drew his great weight up from his lobby seat he made me nervous. KGB eyes. People who worked in almost any of the old Communist administrations in Russia have these terrible blank eyes that look straight through you and bear no relation whatever to the kind of expressions they try to put on the rest of their faces. Their smiles become a hideous mask, distorting the natural relief of their features – an agonised grimace. Decades of systematic lying have extinguished any kind of sparkle there might ever have been in the windows to their blackened souls.

He rested his hand in the small of my back to lead me out of the hotel and the doorman shrugged at me in resignation. As the only lone woman staying in the Camino Real I was the subject of a lot of professional attention. KGB's car was a vast, black, brand new and gleaming Jeep Cherokee with windows so dark that from outside, even during the day, you would not be able to see if there was anyone in the thing or not. He shot a signal at it as we approached and its lights flashed and locks clunked in welcome. He opened my door and helped me far too attentively up into the cool leather seat. The engine roared into action and Mozart joined us in spirit from the stereo as the little lights flashed to tell us the temperature in and outside the car, to remind us to put our seatbelts on and to inform us of our angle to the terrain. It was freezing in this thing and it smelt of candyfloss. I got goose bumps and hugged myself. KGB Eyes pulled his mobile phone out of its leather case and switched it off. There was a loud and authoritative thud as the central locking clicked in.

'Where jew wan to go?' he grimaced.

'I've only been to one bar so far in the whole city,' I told him. 'So, anywhere is great.'

The jeep purred out of the parking lot, gliding over the ravaged roads and slipping in and out of the whirling traffic. From the chilly heights of this vehicle, the scraggy people darting about on the pavements selling flowers and *pupusas* seemed miles away. *Pupusas* are tortillas with cheese baked into them. You split them open so that the hot cheese runs down your fingers and you stuff pickled vegetables into their middles before burning the roof of your mouth with them. Superb. Everything was darkened by the glass in the windscreen and looked unreal – a projected backdrop to some hi-tech theme park ride. We drove up the hill into the Colonia Escalon, an area in which people don't go out on to the streets without their drivers or bodyguards. Security guards smoked sullenly at the doors and lights flickered in the imposing porches. Just up here was the Hotel El Salvador. Uncomprehending, as these types always are, of my desire for local colour, he had brought me to a flash western hell-hole, indistinguishable from the Camino Real except the pool's bigger at the El Salvador.

Everyone here seemed to know my new friend and his very presence had people obsequiously scraping about and muttering to each other behind the scenes. I ordered a margarita and he, suspiciously, ordered ice water. I hate teetotallers. We took our drinks on a tour of the hotel's pool area and he led me on to a dark balcony that had views over the whole of San Salvador. The stars were bright and low and I peered around for the waning Hale Bop comet. He, repulsively, was looking through the darkness at me as the city swayed and sparkled below.

'So what was the position you held during the war?' I asked innocently, trying to pretend I had once known but it had slipped my mind.

So he hadn't actually been the President, but he was in the right-wing Arena party and had been extremely senior *indeed*. Now he was a businessman. In those days he had flown backwards and forwards and had perhaps been involved in the running of the army and the progress of the war. I ordered another margarita. He played with his straw and explained, occasionally blinking his dead eyes, how terribly misrepresented the government had been during the conflict. All those atrocities? Mostly committed by the rebels on their own people to make the government look bad. All those journalists murdered? Some, he conceded, may have been caught in cross-fire but for the most part they too were killed by guerrillas to discredit the government in the eyes of the western press. He had hurtled on to the defensive before I had even asked a question.

As he gave long and utterly mendacious accounts of endless specific incidents which the world misreported but which he alone fully understood ('Jew see? Our soldiers coont haff bin there at dees time so eet was opfiously de FMLN') I switched off and started thinking about how hot and cross Dad would have looked in a press conference given by this bloke. Slouched in a chair much too small for him, chewing Nicorettes, tapping his trainers on the lino, running his fingers through his hair, sighing loudly, fidgeting childishly and kicking the chair in front of him to try and rustle up some solidarity in his boredom.

I licked the salt off my lip. KGB was summing up the reasons why only the guerrillas could possibly have killed my father and the six Jesuit priests who had been killed the day before him. (Government soldiers had eventually been convicted of the murder of the latter but my new friend was seemingly unaware of the fact that I might know this. Being blonde and female can help when trying to cajole egomaniacal fascists into saying really stupid things.) The bites on my ankles were itching and I kept leaning down to dab alcohol on them. My inattention finally dawned on my droning companion and he paid flourishingly as though there was simply no end to his magnanimity.

Back in the icy chill of his hearse (oh, well, OK, Jeep) he told me how you had to do what you could to improve the world and love God. The doors clunked into locked-absolutely-no-escape mode. 'Child protection lock. Door cannot be opened from the inside when the system is engaged.' He put his hand under my hair and squeezed the back of my neck. Even at this stage I assumed he was just being Latin and physical. I couldn't believe that a fat man old enough to be my grandfather might actually imagine that I would want to have sexual intercourse with him. I crossed my legs away from him, held on to the handle in the ceiling and looked out of the window.

'Nice area,' I said. He switched the music off.

Back at the hotel he pulled up ten yards from the doorway and didn't undo the central locking. He reached over to kiss me goodbye and ducked my cheek kiss to catch me on the mouth. I pulled away but he failed, in his bottomless pit of arrogance, to notice my reticence. He unclunked the doors and I hopped out. 'I'll geeev jew a reeng later eef I haff time,' he called. It was 10.30.

I ran up to my room and phoned Tom, suffering from post-traumatic shock. 'Hey! I just got sexually harassed by ———!' I said. 'I'm coming over.'

Tom and the lovely Gene Palumbo were enraptured by my experience. Palumbo is another western journalist who took a great interest in Dad, read the pieces about him I had brought with me and said Dad was the kind of journalist he aspired to be. He took me to a vegetarian restaurant for mango juice and soup one afternoon.

To them, from their semi-native point of view, my evening was equivalent to my having been locked in a car by a popstar or something. 'That guy is scum,' pretty much summed up the views of all, and they loved hearing about his, at best, blind and deluded interpretation of wartime events. The idea of my accepting his advances and actually sleeping with this repulsive creature fuelled their imagination and the three of us sat sweating, drinking beer and laughing hysterically under Tom's fluorescent kitchen light.

Later Gene gave us a lift in his tank (I think it was a tank) to La Ventana where we sat in the dark heat on the porch and ate omelettes. At 1 a.m. it was packed with people talking and jostling, although the palm-lined street outside was totally empty, not another light for hundreds of yards in both directions, just crickets screaming. I told Tom about my endlessly hectic love life and he told me about the war. He pestered me for more detail about my hideous encounter. Finally I was interesting in my own right – I had a Salvador story to tell that they didn't already know. Now I felt just like Dad, one of the hacks hanging out at the bar, except that he always had the best stories. Always lit up the seedy room.

Letter of condolence from Marie Natanson, November 1989
You don't me and probably never heard of me – but I've heard so much about you. Your father spoke of you constantly.

I'm a television producer with the Canadian Broadcasting Corporation and I first met your father in Jerusalem during the summer of 1982.

I had just finished an assignment in Beirut and was relaxing at the American Colony Hotel in Jerusalem chatting with other journalists when the word went round that your father was arriving. I couldn't understand why everyone was so excited and happy at the prospect of yet another journalist joining us, but when I met your father I understood.

I'd been eating oysters at the Occidental Bar and Grill in Washington, DC on Walter Ellis's birthday in 1987. In those days, before his recent marriage, he was always depressed and Dad ordered a slice of chocolate cake with a candle in it from the bar to cheer him up.

I went out for dinner at Jo Allen's with Walter before I left for El Salvador and he told me a story about how Dad had once come over to visit him in Berlin. On their first night out together, mates from the same paper who had met in the Northern Irish troubles when they were swilling whisky at the Europa Hotel, Dad went home with Walter's girlfriend, Evelyn. Evelyn was tall and German and lived with Dad for a few years in New York in a tiny flat on 27th and 2nd that had views over the whole of Manhattan. She pore a poncho in the winter and liked very very hot Indian food.

She jumped over puddles, refused to run Dad's baths for him and laughed at his angst. I liked Evelyn. I didn't realise she was stolen property.

As well as spending my life bumping into women who have known my father, I also run into a lot of cuckolded men. In 1992 I was working for an American TV company in Moscow and when I told the correspondent my name his face contorted with displeasure. Over the ensuing months I discovered that my father had sloped away from the White House press dinner in 1980 with the love of this man's life, Shirley Huang. 'I met him at the bar, of course,' she told me. 'I was . . . gee . . . I must have been . . . twenty-three.'

Dinner with Walter in Jo Allen's depressed me. I was beginning to dislike Dad, and to feel that my sentimentality about him existed just because I was his daughter, and that if I met him in some bar tomorrow I would see a sleazy, drunken hack who stole his best friends' girlfriends and hung around all night at revolting bars.

I was picking at my oriental chicken salad and wondering why I had wasted so much of my life missing Dad so much, why I couldn't have the kind of father who arrives home at 5.30 with a newspaper under his arm, kisses his wife and polishes his train set. I glanced across the table I had sat at with Dad a few years before. 'Let's go to Jo Allen's,' he had said. 'I hate Jo Allen's.'

I think I had the chicken salad then, actually. He had a burger and ate it irritably, wanting to go home. I could see him, clearly, sipping his martini, waving his hand in the air to demonstrate the shape of the lemon twist he required, but I couldn't get enough distance from him to tell what I might think of him now.

'In every generation there's one person with the Achilles option,' said Walter. 'Your dad had it.'

I chewed on. 'But how could you ever forgive him for going home with Evelyn?' I asked, trying to prompt him into venom. 'I wouldn't have.'

Walter's face dropped. He could see that I hadn't perceived the overwhelming love with which he had told the story. It had fallen, he feared, on unsympathetic ears. 'I don't believe that, Anna!' he said, turning to me urgently. 'He was so wonderfully charismatic you forgave him everything,' smiled Walter, genuinely worried that my opinion of Dad might be marred. 'He was a very sad man,' he said. 'But you didn't see it often.'

I think though that people did see it. I think that's why women wanted to look after him and why men found him immediately sympathetic. In his obituary to Dad in the *Sunday Times*, journalist Cal McCrystal wrote: 'Yet Blundy's heroic (how he would hate that word) exploits attracted sustained acclaim, from Middle East war to factional conflict, especially in his beloved Lebanon. After spells there he would return gloomily to regale his editors with anecdote in one hand and Martini in the other, before declaring: "I'm not going back to that shit-hole. Should I? What d'you think? Perhaps I should write a book on Gaddafi?" (He did).'

I think the slight sadness showed in all Dad's indecision and eagerness for advice and I love the reference here to what he would think of Cal's choice of words. Like every word I speak or write, all those obituaries were written

with the spectre of my irreverent and cliché-eschewing
father looking over their shoulders. 'But no grave will
inter his reputation as one of Britain's best narrators of war
and other social and political ineptitudes. No editor who
knew him will bury his or her grief. No journalist will dis-
pose of his memory.' Certainly not this one, anyway.
Every time I nearly write a *Sunday Times*ish sentence with
a dropped intro – 'It was not the noise of the engines nor
the lights on the control panel. The pilot knew his plane
was going down when . . .' – or lapse into pomposity –
'He was the quintessence of all things Russian . . .' – I see
a smirk and a scowl and I leap at the top right-hand button of the keyboard. Delete.

I knew Walt was right. Suddenly, rather than an over-
bearing lech lurking on a bar stool, I saw my dad turning
up in Berlin, tired, awkward, not quite sure what he was
doing there. He didn't seem to have the faintest clue why
women liked him and was always stunned by their
impressive qualifications and their baffling interest in slime
like him. 'She's an acrobat!', 'She works for the State
Department!', 'She went to Harvard!', 'She was on the
cover of *Vogue*!'

I, waiting by the phone, counting cars on the street,
compared myself to them. I'm not at all supple, I thought.
I'm not old enough to be a lawyer. I'll never get into a
good university. I have goofy teeth and a cleft chin and I'll
never be that beautiful. Dad, unfortunately, was honest. I
possessed one item of clothing in nineteen years on which
he complimented me. It was a long bright yellow dress
with a white lace collar and it had little blue, green and red
teapots dotted all over it. Dad loved it. 'Why don't you
ever wear that teapot dress any more?' he would whine

almost every time he saw me, years after I had outgrown the thing. 'That's revolting.' 'Why do you wear things like that?' 'It's ridiculous', he would say about everything else. I was crestfallen and defiant.

When I was about twelve we went out for tea at the Waldorf with a friend of mine called Zizi and my stomach knotted in agony when Dad said he thought she was beautiful. She is beautiful (even more so now) and I think he meant to compliment me by saying something nice about my friend. I was destroyed. If my own father thought Zizi better looking than me, what hope was there of ever seducing her brother? (Actually, it turned out to be somewhat easier than anticipated.)

Letter of condolence from Zizi Durrance, November 1989
Last night after I heard of what had happened I remembered sitting in Chapel at Queenswood. Generally it was so boring, but one particular reading always moved me. It was about a man walking through a desert alone and he noticed footprints in the sand next to him, and when he was desperate for food or drink and needed help he noticed that they were no longer there. He turned to God and said, 'Lord why when I needed you were you not there?' And God replied, 'I was. I was carrying you.'

Dad told me he loved one woman's hair, another's teeth.

'But then you have to go shopping with them and it's so fucking boring. It's so much more fun with you or Ben,' he said, actually stumped by the conundrum. So I was the ugly interesting one, who could tell a joke but was dispatched before the evening dresses needed to be

donned. I hated him for not seeing these women's limita-
tions (usually defined by me as idiocy and artifice) and
couldn't believe he had been sucked in by such crass
deceptions. Of course, in retrospect, I see it was they not
he who had been sucked into something that didn't really
exist. When he died there was a song on the radio all the
time with a line that went 'It's a tragedy for me to see the
dream is over', and that's how he seemed. I always kind of
knew that he might not turn up the next time, that what
he offered was tenuous and fragile. That if I blinked at the
wrong moment it might all disappear.

The next morning at 11 a.m. there was a knock on the
door of my room. I squinted through the peep-hole and
there, smiling lasciviously, was my new friend with the
air-conditioned car, in a freshly pressed white sports shirt.

'Ay thought ay might surprise jew!' he announced to
the room number.

'Hang on. I'm not dressed. Down in a sec.' I scowled.

I would have liked to called security, but I had asked
him if he might be able to get me into the Rosales hospital, so civility was obligatory. I was embarrassed to want to
go at all and felt that my interest might seem morbid and
sick even to the sickest of escorts, so I wore a white dress
and combed my hair back into an efficient ponytail.

I was dreading going in so much that the drive to the
hospital seemed much too short. When I had initially
mentioned the Rosales to Eros, that first evening I arrived,
he had thrown his head back and laughed. 'Oh man! The
Rosales! That place during the offensive, man!' He puffed
his cheeks out and blew. 'That where they took your old
man?'

When we got there and had been sufficiently stared at by the barefooted people outside, it turned out that the tiniest glance from my companion was enough to have the uniformed security guard hauling back the heavy gates and smiling cloyingly. Waiting outside in the hope of seeing their loved ones were women in red and white dresses with matching plastic jewellery and faces glowing with sweat. There were men with gold teeth in straw hats and very old, very tight T-shirts. A Toyota pulled up with a screaming, bleeding man in the back and we all went through together into the Unidad del Emergencias. The man stopped screaming and passed out.

The place stank. Despite the shady corridors open on to palmy courtyards, the heat was overwhelming and people with festering, untreated wounds were lying around on the floor and on trolleys waiting to be seen. Here was the red dust I had seen Dad wheeled through on the ITN news that night, and here were the beleaguered student doctors and nurses whose colleagues had tried to treat him. It had seemed so unbelievably far away then, but here it was. Just a shitty, underfunded, underdrugged third world hospital where people die from appendicitis and post-operative infections. Where you can smell iodine, urine and blood.

All the patients looked forlorn and pleading, out of place in this grand colonial edifice with its statues, fountains and bright green fronds gleaming in the sunlight.

My father was discharged from the Rosales on 17 November at 10.55 a.m. 'Special reasons for discharge – incapacitated for.' Interesting euphemism for dead: 'Incapacitated for discharge.' A bit like 'unsatisfactory patient care outcome' or something. He had suffered 'bilateral pulmonary lesion plus lesion to dorsal vertebrae caused by firearm'. At 8.15 a.m. he had undergone an operation which was successfully completed. He died almost immediately afterwards of two cardiac arrests.

He was terrified of dying of a heart attack. I have seen the cardiogram printouts of the event, with the regular rise and fall of a normal heartbeat zigzagging up and down the middle band of the graph, suddenly punctuated by an awful spasmodic mountain range of squiggle, defacing the page of green quadratic paper and signifying a burst of agonising pain. A struggle? A cry? A gasp for breath? Maybe. And here it was recorded on this fading document for his daughter to see nearly a decade later. Here was his death, logged and filed.

The British Embassy attaché Iain Murray, who had briefed Dad the night before on the situation in San Salvador, had stood outside the door of the operating theatre, desperately trying to arrange to have him moved. 'He came in the evening he arrived and I told him "keep your head down", or something. The best you can say about it is, he was unconscious,' he told me. He had sent out to a nearby hospital for vital drugs – they couldn't perform the operation on Dad without them – and his wife gave blood. Dad's condition was too dire for transfer and Murray was told he would have to wait until after the operation, then, perhaps, there might be some improvement. When Murray heard that Dad had survived the procedure he called Dad's editor at the *Correspondent*, cautiously optimistic. Jon Connell remembers the phone call.

When I telephoned Connell myself to tell him I was going to El Salvador he said, 'Why can't you write about cooking? Don't you fucking learn, you Blundys?' He said he had gone off to a little place round the corner for lunch that day and when he got back there was a message that Dad had been shot.

'It was typical David in a way. Most people would have been happy with what they'd got, but he'd wanted to go and check again. I always let him do kind of what he wanted because we knew it was a great coup to have got him on to the *Correspondent* in the first place.'

Tom Gibb of the *Financial Times* also stood outside the door of the operating theatre. Also gave blood. 'I think there were some girls there who had been with him. I was in a state of shock.' *Fecha y hora de defunción* – 10.55 a.m.

I was in the taxi on the way to Heathrow when the *defunción* finally occurred, when the squiggles appeared on the paper. Now I shuffled around past the student doctors and nurses of the Rosales, twittering to the obese lech by my side. 'Where is the morgue?' I asked him, breezily. Where, I wondered, is the place where they stole Dad's Rolex and rifled through his pockets? 'Jew don't want to see that,' he stated. Good point, I supposed.

I smiled at my blank-eyed companion as he pointed out the emergency operating theatres where Dad would have been taken (hot, yellowing cubbyholes with ancient padded trolleys, rusting equipment and flickering fluorescent lights) and I cheerfully took some pictures. 'Lovely chapel,' I beamed, raising the camera to my eyes.

I was thinking about my Aunt Pauline and her practical nursing attitude towards hospitals. No clammy terror strikes her at the thought of resuscitation equipment.

She lives, Dad's sister, in Voorheesville, Albany, New York State. This, for all its proximity to beautiful lakes and mountains, is real suburban America – white slatted houses in little estates, neat lawns of thick-bladed olive green grass, mailboxes marked with the name of each family, mosquito screens, electric barbecues, skateboards and remote-controlled garage doors.

Dad always seemed painfully out of place there. Everything he did was a mess. He would slump into the red leather sofa, drape a leg over one of its arms and light a cigarette. I bet he was the only person ever allowed to smoke in that house. His jeans looked scrumpled, his hair looked ruffled, his expensive shirts suddenly wanted an iron and needed doing up a bit more effectively. His bag was scraggy and smelt of cigarettes and airports and no matter how hard he tried he couldn't get the towels back on the towel rails the way they were supposed to be. He was too big, too long, too shambolic. He didn't fit.

Dad and the sister who, fifteen years older than him, had played a huge part in his early upbringing, always had appallingly morbid conversations. I think it must have been partly to do with the fact that she worked nights. She would sleep all day with the curtains closed and a white noise box crackling into the room to drown out the day. Pauline talked about her heart patients and Dad talked about his symptoms – palpitations, slight headache, occasional nausea, vague tiredness after strenuous exertion, that kind of thing. She would tell him there was nothing wrong with him, but just to be on the safe side she tended to suggest cardiograms, CAT scans and all sorts of other procedures that were more likely than anything to frighten Dad into an early grave.

After these conversations he and I would usually slope off to the neatest mall so that he could find somewhere to

have a martini and I could have donut. 'Heesville!' he
would exclaim as we arrived in the chilly splendour of
Crossgates mall (twenty-eight-screen cinema, forty burger
joints, a Macy's and lots of places to buy garden furniture).
He would rap his fingers up and down on my shoulder in
boredom as we walked and clout me round the ear at my
every choice of dream outfit. 'Hey! Buy me that,' I'd say,
pointing out a boob tube with glittery palm trees on it and
a pair of Lycra hot pants. 'You are repulsive,' he would
reply.

We were lying by the lake once, up near my aunt's
house, and Dad and Pauline were having one of their
isn't-life-grim discussions. My cousin and I dived in off a
raft and Dad came and pretended to be a shark. 'Dum
dum dum dum dum' he sang before submerging himself
in the murky water to grab our legs and drag us under. He
could swim along underwater with me on his shoulders,
slippery as a seal.

'I mean, it's a wonder we make it this far at all,' said
Pauline, who wouldn't go in the water.

'It is,' agreed Dad, spitting a piece of tobacco off the
end of his tongue. We were dripping into the wooden
seats of the restaurant area, waiting for cold Cokes, beers
and Dr Peppers (my choice – 'He's a pepper, she's a pepper, you're a pepper, I'm a pepper, Doctor Pepper!') it
was hot but breezy and big families were unpacking their
cool-boxes and spreading out their beach towels.

'If you think about all the diseases that can get you and
all the accidents you could have,' she went on. 'We're
pretty lucky to be this age.'

But despite her morbidity, Pauline was the one person
at Dad's funeral who had anything upbeat to say. 'There

just has to be more to it than this. I know I'm going to see Mum and Dad, and Mark and David again. Otherwise there would just be no point,' she told me. No, there wouldn't, I agreed.

She is the nearest thing I ever had to a traditional kind of relative. She has never forgotten my birthday and she has never not sent me a Christmas card. She always remembers the names of my boyfriends and is proud of whatever it is I am doing (even when it is writing a column about myself). She actually cared what I wanted for my birthdays when I was little and would remember what I had liked in the malls, which Barbies I already had and what earrings looked nice on me after I had my ears pierced.

I find the slant of her writing (not dissimilar to Dad's) comforting on envelopes, and she is the only relation I have who has always lived in the same place, can be relied upon to still be going out with the same man, cook the same dishes, look after you if you are ill and ask the same kinds of questions. She is the kind of parent everyone wishes for, but is probably irritated by if they have. Her house is full of framed photographs of her sons: graduations, weddings and – soon – christenings.

It is my sister Charlotte now, not me, who receives packages from America full of merchandise from the latest Disney film, not yet out here, and I'm sure she'll be far more grateful one day than I imagine she is now.

Chapter Seven

I hold it true, whate'er befall;
I feel it, when I sorrow most;
'Tis better to have loved and lost
Than never to have loved at all.

1985

Dad met Samira, Charlotte's mum, in Beirut. It was obvious that this was someone special because he talked about her all the time. 'I met a Sudanese woman with a bone through her nose and a grass skirt,' he said. 'She kept building fires to dance round in the hotel,' he explained. They had been staying in the same hotel and had had a courtship based on leaving each other rude messages with the receptionist, as far as I could make out. I would meet her soon, he promised. She was coming back from Beirut. She did. I was summoned to the Zanzibar.

I don't think it exists any more, but it was a horrible American-style cocktail bar in Covent Garden where you had to be a member and where they made martinis how Dad liked them. It was all short-skirted waitresses and cocktail shakers at a time when it was probably the only place in London to achieve the effect.

Dad had clearly warned them on the door what I looked like because they let me straight in and gestured me over to a chrome-gleaming corner.

Dad and Sam were sitting in blue, ultraviolet light, both

Aunt Pauline and Dad

Dad in 1956

Mum and Dad, 1968

Haiti

Bognor Regis, '74

*Dad, cousin Steven and me, Albany,
NY State, 1980*

*Grandpa Fred Blundy,
Auntie Millie and me*

(left) Me and dad

Dad, Charlotte and me, 1988

Dad - the plane had to be landed; he felt sick

Tess

*Christina Kulukundis and me,
Keene Valley, '87*

Dad and Charlotte, Kenwood, '89

Sergei

Me and Mum in Russia, 1992

*Grace Chatto and Charlotte Blundy at
Eurodisney, 1996.*

The bell tower (left) and the Rosales Hospital, El Salvador

*Eros and me at the Camino
Real pool, San Salvador*

Stephen Lucas and me at the party on 24 May 1997.

Horatio

smoking and laughing. She was younger then than I am now, terrifyingly. She was twenty-six, very beautiful and had an extremely posh English accent. Although I had assumed Dad was lying about the bone, I had imagined that she was actually Sudanese. In fact she was half Sudanese, had been brought up in England and had gone to Cambridge. Dad found this wildly impressive. I rolled my eyes.

I showed her some photo-booth pictures of a Goth that I was going out with or wanted to go out with or something, and she didn't laugh. Or at least, not while I was still sitting there. She was funny and clever and I wondered what she was doing with Dad. I probably asked her this. She probably said she didn't know.

They moved in together not very long after the Zanzibar meeting I think, and they seemed to laugh a lot. There were all kinds of engagement and marriage murmurings and Mum, Ricky, newborn Grace and I spent Christmas at their flat.

Having three, and sometimes four, parents seemed fairly normal to me, and it was Dad who on 10 December 1985 came to pick me and my friends Lucy Clift and Clare Adams up from the place where we were photocopying our alternative school magazine to take us to St Mary's, Paddington. My sister Grace had been born to Mum and my stepfather, Ricky.

We stopped to buy champagne and roses and then we piled, all four of us, into the delivery suite, we three girls in our hideous maroon uniforms and Dad in his jeans. Ricky stood at the bedside, pale and shaking. Mum was wrapped in a sheet and still covered in blood. Little Grace lay jaundiced and black-haired in a plastic cot by Mum's side. Dad was captivated.

Diary, 10 December 1985: At last Ricky phoned to say she'd been born and was fine. Phoned everyone I could think of and Dad came over and took us all to the hospital. Mum was fine – tired and bloody – had her totally naturally and said it was the most painful thing ever. Stitches. The baby, Grace, is beautiful, perfect. I held her. She's adorable.

It was odd, although it didn't strike me at the time, that Dad had seen Mum in this state twice. Once at the Whittington in 1970 with his child, me, and now with Gracie fifteen years later. Dad had paced around Waterlow Park smoking, the first time. In those days fathers didn't often go in to watch. He had been hysterical with anxiety because Mum eventually had to have a general anaesthetic and I was forcepsed out. Apparently Dad was standing outside the door while the midwife shouted for an anaesthetist. That's when he took to the park.

Mum and I then lived in lots of insalubrious North London flats from which Dad would occasionally turn up to evict us. 'You're not living here! There are rats!' he would shout, gathering up our stuff in his arms and hurrying us out to his car. His protectiveness quite often took the form of disgust.

Dad cooked the turkey that Christmas in 1985. He brought it in, proudly wearing a purple paper crown. Sam served the sprouts.

This was the beginning of the transformation that was to be completed when Charlotte was born a couple of years later. That turkey was the first thing I had ever known Dad to cook – but it wouldn't be the last. Sam definitely seemed to be a good influence, although whether he was similarly stabilising for her I'm not quite sure. I certainly didn't care. I remember once going skiing with a friend's family and meeting Dad and Samira completely by chance at Heathrow on their way to a wedding in Holland. Dad had been forced to hire white tie and had surpassed even his usual limits of irritation in the organisational frenzy. It was not his friends getting married, he didn't know or like them, he didn't want to wear a top hat and he had altogether better and cheaper things he could have been doing with himself for the weekend, was the message I received. Sam seemed inordinately pleased to see me and took refuge under my ski jacket while Dad hurled himself at the check-in counter in a rage. I was so glad it was her going, not me. He had a knack of making you feel that his bad mood was your fault. But, this time, not my fault!

Sam always seemed to be on my side without being patronising. I once went to a party off Haverstock Hill with a big group of friends who had gathered first outside the Steele's pub where some of us thought we could get served. The party was in the huge house of a famous thinker. It had *chaises-longues*, french windows, stripped floors and overflowing bookcases. The parents were away and the golden floor was littered with darkened huddles of scraggy people, smoking joints, rolling joints, passing joints and loading up bongs. The whole house was very much like the inside chamber of a bong in atmosphere. I walked into two rooms to find people having sex in a semi-clothed, rushed kind of a way. Nobody was friendly, not many people were even talking and there was nothing to drink. I smoked about five joints, lost my friends and started to get very upset and paranoid. The fear, man.

I had told my mum that I was staying the night with a friend so as (a) not to worry her and (b) not to get into trouble but I had lost the friend in the gloom, and it looked as though I would be spending the night here, in the house of hippie death. I crawled around through the dark looking for a phone and eventually interrupted some people lying in front of the television watching *American Werewolf in London* on video for the third time that night. 'This bit really cracks me up.' It was about 1 a.m.

I phoned Dad, desperately hoping Sam would pick up the phone. She did. Snivelling and wheedling, I explained the situation to her. Half an hour later a red Peugeot 504 pulled up outside, driven by Dad. Sam came in to try and find me, knowing that Dad would never let me out of his sight again if he got wind of what perversions were being practised within. It was a successful mission. I got home. I didn't get shouted at. I didn't have to skulk off and have sex with a drug addict.

Basically, Sam tempered Dad's irritation with and disapproval of me and let me smoke when he went out. I seemed to have a real stepmother.

When I was seventeen I went to visit Dad in Washington for the penultimate time. I had short hair and rings, and my boyfriend and I smoked a lot of dope. Dad came to meet me at the airport in his rusting old Mercedes with holes in the floor, and halfway in from the airport he declared that we had already run out of things to say to each other and when I was going home. 'Fuck off,' I said. 'Don't swear,' he replied, groping for his cigarettes.

Samira was heavily pregnant with Charlotte and was waiting for us at their house on T Street, a real Georgetown thing with a wooden porch out back and a gloomy living room. He moved so often that every time I saw him the first thing he would do was show me round. Here, for the first time, I had a room of my own.

Sam and I made lots of salads out of pasta, cream, walnuts and olives, and people came round for dinner. We sat out in the garden to eat. It was balmy and still, sirens screaming in the distance. Alexander Chancellor was there, the Rusbridgers and perhaps Peter Pringle and his wife Eleanor. They laughed a lot and loudly and a racoon came into the garden.

My campaign, while I was in the States, was to be allowed to go and visit my schoolfriend Christina Kulukundis who had a summer house up in the Adirondack mountains near a place called Keene Valley. Christina spent every summer there and it sounded very rights-of-passagey as an experience – nature, drink, drugs and boys. I wanted to go. Sam was pregnant, Dad was irritable (they were looking after an Israeli journalist, Hirsch Goodman's dog, Dotty, who was subsequently poisoned outside Tel Aviv by burglars) and I was a sulky adolescent. They had to be pleased to be rid of me.

They were.

I flew to New York and took a train all the way up the side of Lake Champlain and tried to read *The Cherry Orchard* in Russian. I was the only person getting off at Westport and there didn't seem to be a station to speak of. I leapt down into the dust of a forest clearing and the huge silver Amtrak snake disappeared towards Toronto. There was nobody there to meet me, so I sat on my suitcase and smoked a cigarette, watching the yellow light seep through the trees. A man in shorts came battling out of the undergrowth, scratches on his face and a rucksack on his back. 'Was that the train for Toronto?' he asked, wildly. I told him it had been and he swore and ran back whence he had come.

Half an hour later Christina pulled up in the clearing, statuesque in an old Buick, a black swimming costume and a sarong. Her feet were bare and her hair was wet from swimming under a waterfall. As we drove away she lit a cigarette and told me she had been meeting all the trains from New York that day and that an axe-wielding psychopath had come up to her just after each train had pulled off to ask her if that had been the train for Toronto.

We swung in a hammock on her gleaming white porch, watched humming-birds and drank cans of beer. We were invited to a party.

This, it transpired, involved sitting on a different porch in a different hammock in the dark, drinking vodka and responding when people said, 'Anyone want a bong hit, man?' This was where I met Roger Scott Hudson, a data processor from Texas who had just left the navy. He was twenty-two. He sang the 'dum dum da da dum dums' in the background to my and Christina's rendition of 'Stand By Me'. Roger and I consummated our relationship under the eaves of the vast, creaking house after Christina and I had discovered that even if you spit the vodka directly at each other, completely simultaneously and in an absolutely straight jet, it doesn't meet in the middle and stop – you still get it all over the other person's face.

Diary, 27 August 1987: It was obvious what was going to happen because Roger had his head on my lap and kissed and stroked my hand. I didn't really want to but ended up doing so till I did want to.

In the morning Dad and Samira arrived and checked into a frilly hotel in the town, near the Spread Eagle Inn where the woman asked if you want 'budder or mayo' in your sandwiches. As soon as I had left DC, they decided they needed a holiday too and had elected to follow me up into the hills. Samira was huge and exhausted, waddling around in dresses that weren't quite made for her shape, her tummy protruding through the burst buttons. She was too preoccupied to be interested in my holiday romance and Dad just pretended not to notice the calls to the hotel room. 'Someone called Roger,' he would say, proffering the receiver and plunging back into his newspaper.

Someone Called Roger drove me to lakes and waterfalls in his big rusting car and rolled joints as we trundled past diners, log cabins and shops selling Indian headdresses and silver jewellery. He taught me the phrase 'blue balls' and played me songs by the Grateful Dead.

This was the holiday when everything changed with Dad. He didn't have the power any more. Normally his being grumpy would have devastated me. 'Don't sing,' was all he would have to say to make my heart sink and bring tears to my eyes. I loved to sing, love to sing, and he hated it when I did. 'Why can't you have a clear voice like Linda Ronstadt?' he would ask, idly, not meaning to upset me but wishing I would shut up. I suspect he had slept with Linda Ronstadt.

This time he could fuck off. I was singing to someone

else, who liked it. The fact that Samira was pregnant made me invulnerable. They had their family and their life of which I was demonstrably not a part, and I, all of a sudden, had mine. I even wished them well.

Diary, 28 August 1987: Anyway, had a really good laugh with Dad once we'd left DC. He's such a good bloke. Also got on well with Sam and had a laugh. She can't smoke because of the baby so as soon as Dad left the house to do a radio show or something (he does lots about the Gaddafi book and he's brilliant. Sounds so clever and knowledgeable!) we'd both run for our cigarettes. I think Dad likes Sam more than he'd say. They had a fantastic time in Keene Valley – picnics, walks, etc.

They would go back to the pink-curtained Inn at night to laugh, read and sleep and I, for the first time, didn't have to go and skulk alone in the adjoining room, shut out but kept in tow. Didn't have to wait for Dad to stop smoking and switch the light off, didn't need to wake him up because I felt sick, didn't want his attention.

I was lying under the stars. They dangled out of the sky so low they brushed our noses. Lying stoned, watching for shooting stars, giggling and having sex with Someone Called Roger.

Christina's parents, a little baffled by Dad's shambolic, chain-smoking presence, his dusky pregnant girlfriend and his peculiar charm, invited us all to a posh party up the mountain. Jackie Onassis wasn't actually there, but a lot of her friends almost certainly were. Christina and I, disguised by our summer dresses, youth and suntans, weren't too horrendously out of place, so we drank all the white wine and twittered out on the lawn. Dad and Samira were having more of a problem. Dad was the only person in the light-flooded, pine-clad palace who smoked. He not only smoked but he broke his filters off, dropped them on the floor and then pulled bits of tobacco out of his mouth. And he was wearing jeans. Samira was the only remotely scruffy-looking person there apart from Dad and Charlotte was clearly visible, kicking from under the painfully tight summer dress. Everyone wondered who they were and what they were doing there. Sam started to choke on an olive and had to lie down on the pristine sofa, coughing, spluttering and tearing her dress. Dad, laughing so much he began to cough as well, poured water into her mouth, down her front and all over the floor. We soon left.

Dad and Sam took Christina and me out to dinner at some horrible restaurant in a mall where they brought the iced water in yellow tinted glasses. Christina embarrassed me by talking about drugs and sex, assuming, because of his manner, that Dad was a 'cool parent' who wouldn't object. He didn't object when it was other people's children. He knew, however, that he wouldn't have a leg to stand on if he raised the issue with me, so he just went chilly and bit his tongue. 'Christ, you lot are disgusting,' he spat, pretending it was a joke. But I was free. Say what you like.

Ten of us squeezed into someone's Jeep that night and drove all the way into the valley down dirt tracks, off the edge of precipices and through forests to buy a keg of beer at a bar in town. The boys all had long hair teetering on the edge of becoming dreadlocks, checked shirts and pierced ears. There was an obligatory one guitar for every group of four persons. The only thing anyone could play was 'Stairway to Heaven'. By the keg stage we were already drunk and stoned, so, to liven up the journey, Christina and I ran through a Beatles medley we had prepared earlier.

The party for the evening was held outdoors on a deck that was falling off a mountain. There was a sheer drop to the stars to one side. Some time after midnight, Someone Called Roger perched on the wooden rail in the singing dark and leant forward to clasp his hands behind my bare back. 'You know what, Anna? I think I love you.' He smiled into the heat and I kissed him.

The next day I was consigned to the back of an air-conditioned hire car for the six-hour drive back to Washington, DC. I breathed in Dad's smoke and listened to him bitch behind the wheel, but it wasn't the same as it always had been before. Our relationship would have changed for ever that summer if he had lived. It would have been a turning point in my growing up and away from him if only it hadn't all been snatched back again when he died, making me need him, hopelessly, more than ever. But for now he couldn't break my heart any more, I thought. He was a grumpy old man and I had the rest of my life ahead of me. Obviously, I hadn't anticipated that I was going to wallow in an agony of devastation for a decade without him. Or how I would feel when Charlotte was born.

1988

'I've just got to get something for the Beazle,' said Dad on the way in from the airport. This was my last trip to

Washington – summer 1988, the year before he died – and I had been usurped. I was sleeping in Charlotte, 'The Beazle's' room, but I wasn't allowed to switch the humidifier off – there was something wrong with her breathing. I sweated and writhed all night, listening to her rasp.

Dad's temples were greying and he went to the office in a suit. A nice suit. One that fitted. One of the many he seemed suddenly to have that fitted.

Lewis Chester told my favourite anecdote about Dad in his *Sunday Correspondent* obituary in 1990. Dad's normal attire of leather jacket, jeans, trainers and barely buttoned shirt was not really acceptable at the *Sunday Times* back then, even under Harry Evans, but Dad got away with it. Michael Bateman, editor of the Atticus gossip column for which Dad worked, was not much bothered. But when the headmaster of Eton rang up to say that he refused to believe that the reporter sent to attend to him could conceivably be a representative of the *Sunday Times*, he took action. Dad was forced to go and buy a hideous green suit.

Dad subsequently met Harry Evans in the lift. 'I thought you were told to buy a suit,' said Harry.

'I did,' said Dad.

'Then why aren't you wearing it?' asked the editor.

'I am wearing it, Harry,' Dad replied.

The suit then saw action in the grounds of Willie Whitelaw's house in Cumbria, where Dad had gone snooping through the bushes in pursuit of colour on the then Minister for Northern Ireland. Four policemen manhandled him off to the nearest station. Bateman, who had to talk them into releasing Dad, over the phone, was told by the policemen that the suit's colour had given rise to a suspicion that his reporter might be an IRA man.

★

There was a bottle of aftershave in the bathroom in Washington and there was food in the fridge. Not a packet of Ritz crackers and a bottle of vodka, but real food. Lettuce, tomatoes, ham, different kinds of cheese, packets of expensive coffee, big cartons of orange juice, semi-skimmed milk and hundreds of jars of baby food. The flat quite often smelt more of cooking than of cigarettes. This was not something I had ever encountered before.

In his old black Filofax, that was sent to me from El Salvador when he died, Dad had scrawled notes to himself in amongst the stuff about state departments, embassies and arms dealers. 'Milupa. Baby toothpaste. Harley's rusks. Charlotte – oral polio? Standard dosage.'

When he turned on the stereo in the flat on P Street she would haul herself up to stand right next to the speakers and wiggle and laugh. She sat on his knee and giggled into his face, huge-eyed and unquestioningly trusting. We took her to restaurants and he would quietly, patiently feed her the huge adult plate of food he had ordered for her. She would still be hungry. Ice-cream? The cheese plate? He didn't rap his fingers on the table, smoke frantically, glance around distractedly and sigh periodically like he usually did. She squealed in delight as he pushed her on the baby swings in a Georgetown park and she splashed him wildly in her evening bath.

Unbelievable. It wasn't a girlfriend or a war who finally snaffled him from right under my nose. It was my own beautiful sister. He was constantly angry with me for not loving her enough, for complaining about the humidifier in her room, for saying I couldn't sleep with her snoring, for not doting as much as he did. I sulked. He shouted. He bought me a leather jacket at Banana Republic on Wisconsin. He wanted to get me a sort of feminine-style one with padded shoulders and a nipped-in waist. I wanted one like his – big and brown. I got my way but he said it looked hideous and I didn't really want it any more. But this time the break was copable with. Not too disastrous. I was eighteen and more concerned with being on the phone constantly to my boyfriend, Giles, although I was still not really allowed to talk about that sort of thing in front of Dad. I was trying, and doing pretty well, to replace Dad with a more reliable type of gentleman altogether and was cooing down the phone as often as I could possibly get to it. Dad humphed and crackled the newspaper. I'm not sure he was really as disapproving of me, though, as I tended to be think.

Letter of condolence from Peter Taylor of the 'Sunday Telegraph'
Most people remind us of other people, but David was unlike anyone else I have met. He was a complete original, and, like all his legion of friends, I shall miss him dreadfully. He often mentioned you in our conversations here over a beer or two (more usually a vodka martini up with a twist) and I know how proud he was of you.

He really changed after Charlotte was born. He became more focused, more responsible, tenser, more angular and, to his horror, older. He didn't want to make the same mistakes twice.

He planned to move back to London to be near her,

was writing a book about Lockerbie, thought he might take out a pension scheme, look to the future.

Letter, September 1989
I met His Royal Highness the Prince of Wales at the British Embassy last week. Nice. We chatted away for hours. Actually it only felt like hours. It was really for about 18 seconds. He made a very funny speech which he didn't write.

I went to Boston to interview a perfidious slime-ball Greek writer who has made millions writing novels and had some story idea about the deputy prime minister of Greece. Frankly who gives a bucket of flying rat's numbers? Why am I working for the *Sunday Telegraph*? Why am I living in poofter heaven? Why is the Beazle in London? What is life?

I need to write a book and make a lot of money. If that stinking dwarf Greek can do it and have a house in Boston and an apartment, made entirely of glass, overlooking Central Park then I can too. I was thinking that if I had said that Colonel Gaddafy was lower than dog dirt and had intimate relations with camels and carried a copy of *Hustler* magazine inside his Koran he might have me put on his death list like that Salman Rushdie and I would have sold more than three copies of the book.

It seemed so unfair on Charlotte, throwing her rose on to the coffin from her tiny hand, not to have all those silly jokes, fraught last-minute stand-by holidays and suitcase-fuls of stupid presents. No stickers bearing the faces of crazed dictators, posters from losing election campaigns, ivory bracelets, elephant-hair bangles, real Mexican jumping beans with flies that eventually hatch, Ethiopian silver, cotton from cotton farms, stuffed baby alligators carrying briefcases, seal fur cuddly toys, Indian leather moccasins, real voodoo dolls packed in straw with a spell book by their side, shell casings, bullets, pieces of shrapnel, volcanic dust in a jar, prehistoric crocodile teeth and desert roses.

But somehow, she seems to have been genetically programmed to behave as though she did receive them, to act as if he had been there, whispering in her ear all her life while she sang in school nativity plays, coloured in drawings, ran races and fed caged animals. Now nine, she looks just like her father and is the tallest in her class by at least three inches (that's including the boys). She has the same coarse dark hair as him, the same naughty look on her face, the same boredom threshold, the same curiosity and the same devastating charm. Everyone loves her, falls in love with her, is devoted to pleasing her, even when she's being a pain in the arse. People who meet her worry that she might not like them. She reduced one of my boyfriends to tears because she was too dismissive of him, and the others who have met her spent every second of the encounter agonising over what might entertain her most.

She is clever, quick, ironic and funny, mischievous and tireless. She also gives the best advice. I once asked her why she thought someone I fancied kept ignoring me. She paced along Piccadilly, holding my hand and looking fixedly ahead. I assumed she hadn't heard or wasn't interested. Eventually she stopped walking and glanced up. 'I expect he's just shy,' she concluded. She was right. She was five.

The other day we were doing cartwheels on the Heath and she asked after an ex of mine.

'Well, it just went all wrong. He was ill, then he was mad, then he had work problems. One thing after another, you know. Sad though,' I explained as quickly as possible, heading for the ponds. She was all the keener to swim in them when someone told her they were always dredging dead bodies out.

Again we were hand in hand, this time on Hampstead High Street, she in little shorts and a white crop top, looking about thirty. She had been mulling the matter over all day while we watched our melanomas grow and contracted rare diseases from the pond water. 'I suppose the fact that things kept going wrong means you weren't really right for each other in the first place,' she said sunnily. I hadn't thought about it like that before.

Charlotte has inherited a morbid imagination. She's always asking what would happen if that tree fell over, if that building toppled, if the car veered off the road. 'We'd be fine,' I tell her. 'I'm here.' Then she will run through all the possibilities and all my potential failures as a saviour, satisfied only when I admit, 'Well, I suppose if the brakes failed here and I was suddenly paralysed and that lorry crossed the central reservation and we drove into fog all at the same time – then, yes, we would all die.' 'Thought so,' she nods, turning the corners of her mouth down. Just like Dad.

When she was three I took her to Trafalgar Square to feed the pigeons. They landed in her hair, on her shoulders and all over her arms. She burst into tears, clung to me and begged to be taken away. I shooed the pigeons off and dragged her to the edge of the square. She wiped her eyes and grinned up at me. 'Again!' she squealed, eyes twinkling, and headed back to the fray, little white socks flashing through the tourists' legs.

As well as being like Dad, she always reminds me of myself when I was her age, in her precociousness and unwitting sophistication incongruous with her years.

She also has a great relationship with her mum, as I had with mine. They behave like argumentative sisters or flat-mates, bickering and teasing, but totally devoted. Charlotte will insist on the balsamic vinegar dressing. 'Ponce!' shouts Samira. 'You are!' cackles Charlotte.

The Beazle is philosophical about Dad, although her face lights up when I tell her about how he gave her shoulder rides, fed her ice-cream, took her to the zoo. 'Did I scream being that high up?' she asks. 'No,' I tell her. 'You laughed.' 'Was he as tall as that man?' 'Taller.' I was driving her to my house from her home in Clapham once, when she was about six or seven, and she said, 'I wish Daddy was here.' I told her I bet he wished he was too and she sighed and looked out at the rain. 'Still,' she chirped. 'We can't have everything we want in life, can we.'

Sage-like, she opened her bag of crisps and hummed a Spice Girls tune. She has inherited Dad's peculiar ability to have an overview.

El Salvador, 1997

When I got home from the Rosales that day, Eros and Tom came to sit by the pool. Eros was drowsy and spoke even less than usual. He looked pale (comparatively speaking) and had bags under his eyes. 'Are you OK?' I asked him as we went down in the lift after changing.

'Dude,' he confirmed, nodding and shuffling his feet in

his sandals. 'I kind of ate something last night,' he shrugged.

I offered him some Peptobismol or Milk of Magnesia tablets (I have medication for all common, and many not so common, ailments in my black leather wash bag). He declined, laughing. 'No, man. Not that kind of thing. I ate like these hash cakes. I don't know what they put in them, man, but they was *strong*,' he chortled, slinging his towel over his shoulder.

The sun was searing and I had a headache. Tom and Eros drank cold beers and stared straight ahead, having butch conversations. Eros swam, bobbing up occasionally at the edge of the pool, shaggy headed and sleek as an otter. Someone was hammering pieces of corrugated iron together behind the pool hut and I flinched at every thud. 'You know what they do in Northern Ireland, man?' asked Eros of Tom.

'What do they do in Northern Ireland?' queried his friend, twitching ironically.

'They have these like metal plates that they like put behind your kneecaps, man, before they shoot you so the bullet can like ricochet back and smash it in two places!" He lifted his own knee to demonstrate the position of the plate and made his hand into a gun.

'That is some fucking sick shit,' he laughed, squinting into the sun.

'It's fucked up,' said Tom. 'Clever, but fucked up.'

I inquired what their problem was, to be amused by that shit. 'I just think it's amazing all the different ways people can have to be mean to each other, man,' explained Tom.

This led to a discussion about the death squads during the conflict and how the government troops had been brainwashed into performing torture and slow murder.

'They used to make everybody do a little bit so that they were all in it together. Like they'd all have to rape her or like all have to chop a bit off. That way there was this fucked-up camaraderie,' said Eros, swigging at his beer and half-smiling. Tom talked about the fact that the soldiers routinely raped their male victims as well as their female ones. 'It's like the ultimate insult. The ultimate seizure of power.' Corpses were apparently found all over the capital with their pants round their ankles and their heads by their sides. 'You know,' said Eros. 'It's the government soldiers I feel sorry for now. How can they get back to normal life when they know they did all that, man? Lotta suicides.'

They were fascinated, they said, by the depths to which human beings could stoop. I think, although I certainly didn't say so until the next evening when I'd had more to drink, that there is a certain naivety in that. To find human vileness fascinating, there has to be a fundamental belief that most people are not simply vile in the first place. You have to be surprised by their revoltingness.

What's fascinating is the extent to which most people live in relative harmony most of the time. I think it's surprising that more people aren't chopping off each other's noses and bayoneting their neighbours' children.

Anyway, I scowled at the tip of the straw in my empty Coke glass until the subject got changed. 'So, how was the Rosales with lover boy?' asked Tom, and Eros cackled.

'Yeah, it was OK,' I said, pulling at my sarong. 'It wasn't as bad as I expected. It was, you know, a third world hospital. I think I imagined dead people lining the corridors, but it wasn't so awful. I mean, I wouldn't wish it on anyone I knew, but . . .'

'But, it's all right for *them*,' spat Eros. 'Jesus, I hate that attitude, you know? It's like, who cares about the Salvadoreans. I wouldn't want it but they're probably used to it.'

That wasn't what I had meant at all, but Eros really hated me today and I couldn't be bothered to argue. 'That's the one,' I said and dived into the pool. When I got out he was getting ready to leave.

Really, of course, he was just being defensive about a place that is difficult to love, and which he loves. Salvador is dirty and poor and war-ravaged, but Dad as well as Eros found it less depressing than an English seaside town or a suburban cul-de-sac. I do too. Here, in the face of unimaginable adversity, people were dealing with the fundamental problems of life and death, not whether or not supermarkets should be open on a Sunday. Dad loved that and he always found something funny and peculiar to write about. His pieces from war zones were invariably about the life side of death, rather than the horror of it.

The 'Sunday Telegraph' 26 March 1989
Among the millions of Salvadorans who voted in the Presidential elections last weekend was a curious figure: an elderly Englishman in a neat white shirt and a peaked cap, who would look more at home on the Sussex Downs than on the gusty streets of San Salvador.

John Boursot, a small, rather fragile man with a few strands of grey hair, is known locally as Don Juan. He is 75, was born in Sussex, grew up in South Kensington and has lived in El Salvador since 1944.

He has joint British/Salvadoran citizenship and has worked for 19 years as the curator of reptiles at the zoo in San Salvador, the country's capital . . . It is a sorry, neglected place, and, according to Mr Boursot a fitting symbol of modern Salvador. 'It is really the zoo of death . . . everything seems to die here.'

The crocodile poked its nose through the green slime of its pond and Mr Boursot prodded the snout with a metal pole. The crocodile sprang to life, brushing its head and snapping at the sprightly Mr Boursot. 'Poor old chap. Thought he might be getting his lunch,' he said.

I meant to go to the zoo in San Salvador myself to check up on the ancient Boursot, but I never made it.

Chapter Eight

Be near me when my light is low,
When the blood creeps, and the nerves prick
And tingle; and the heart is sick,
And all the wheels of Being slow.

London, 1990

Dad's memorial service was held on 24 January. This is when you're supposed to have stopped grieving and started feeling ready to celebrate the life of the deceased. I wore an olive green suit with huge shoulder pads. ('You can brighten it up after the service with a silk scarf,' said the sales assistant) and I had had my long hair waved. St Bride's was apparently too small, so we held it at St Martin-in-the-Fields in Trafalgar Square. It was packed.

I barely remember the day at all apart from that. I remember walking up into the pulpit to read, and seeing over a thousand people swimming in front of me. I remember taking a breath and realising I was going to have to make this mean something. And suddenly, as I read it, it seemed poignant, briefly. The tears stopped and my hands stopped shaking.

To every thing there is a season, and a time to every purpose
*   under the heaven:*
A time to be born, and a time to die;
A time to plant, and a time to pluck up that which is planted;

A time to kill, and a time to heal;
A time to break down, and a time to build up;
A time to weep, and a time to laugh;
A time to mourn, and a time to dance;
A time to cast away stones, and a time to gather stones
    together;
A time to embrace, and a time to refrain from embracing;
A time to get, and a time to lose;
A time to keep, and a time to cast away;
A time to rend, and a time to sew;
A time to keep silence, and a time to speak;
A time to love, and a time to hate;
A time of war, and a time of peace.

(Ecclesiastes 3:1–8)

I sobbed through 'Jerusalem' and snivelled as my step-father, Ricky, played Bourée 1 and 2 from Bach's Suite No. 3 (something Dad was forever pestering him to play for him because he liked it; Ricky was always too shy). Ben Macintyre read, Marvell's 'To His Coy Mistress' on which Dad had written a thesis in Bristol – 'Had we but world enough and time . . .' – and Harry Evans and Magnus Linklater talked about Dad and his work. He would have been staggered by the number of people there, the extent of the grief and the kind of people who showed up. I don't remember noticing the guests at the time, but reading through the newspaper reports now, I am amazed myself: Eve Pollard, Donald Trelford, Alan Rusbridger, Tina Brown, Trevor McDonald, Jon Snow, John Witherow, Emma Soames, Lord Fitt and all kinds of people I had no idea he knew. Perhaps he didn't.

Dad's friend from university, the poet, Bill Scammell,

read a poem he had written for Dad. It's called 'China to Peru', and the end is making me cry now, sitting in my boyfriend's aunt's house in the Lake District. It has this effect every time I read it. It wasn't just my fingers he was always slipping through. It was everyone's. All the people there, sitting, rustling in St Martin-in-the-Fields. Quietly thinking their thoughts in their black coats as the bright day thundered by unnoticed outside. Beautiful weeping women, robust red-eyed men.

What possible muse
can I summon, Dave?
The muse of the news?
She's all we have,
a groupie; with intent to loiter
about the knees of Magnum and Reuter.

Her usual fee
for a story is
a ride in a taxi
and several corpses,
one or two drinks,
one or two laughs
to wipe away the photographs.

Gene Delacroix
in gay Paree
said her name was fair
as Liberty.
Her stocking tops, her feverish eye
taught the unlettered how to cry.

Anna Blundy

Great magnates love
to have her around:
her favours lingered
all weekend
like musk oil, with a waltz-time dash
of old Vienna's heated flesh.

Your six feet two
of irreverence
seldom knew how to
bow to the dance
of art, or love. You'd prefer
the low mimesis of the bar

whose winking lights
and golden spirit
were all the thoughts
you thought we'd merit
on judgement day, great deadline, when
we'd order true oblivion.

Knee-deep in bills,
old parking tickets,
terminally ill
with rust and rickets
your car moves off. Some assignation
with Arab-Israeli desperation;

some rage for order
where things go leprous
in Salvador;
or your obstreperous

campaign against all staying put,
whether in bed, or in the heart.

You flew off bullish to Washington's stews
with a suitcase fullish
of dirty clothes . . .
Sad emblem! And a funny one too.
A sixteen collar, a size twelve shoe,

some cotton T-shirts,
some fags and pens –
this was your congress
against pretence
and adjectives, and bullshit stories
leaking out from nature's tories.

I hardly dare
mention your jumbo
warmth of feeling
and love of a bimbo.
In fact I won't. You'd tell me, 'Billy
stop being so fucking silly!

I'm late for the shuttle,
late for the hearse.
You just rattle your crappy verse –
I've got an appointment. See you.' Sure,
Dave. Soon, in the Zanzibar.

Afterwards, a cold walk across Trafalgar Square – and drinks. A lot of my friends came, and we all got extremely drunk at the Reform Club where Harry Evans kindly held a reception (ironically, for Dad would never have been let past the doorman). Now it had become a party and I wasn't the hostess. There were people there, friends of Harry's who didn't even know I was David's daughter. I felt strange, left out and drunk.

That night, newly rich, I took some friends out to dinner at ZenW3 in Hampstead and we sat at a big round table and talked about other things as the food spun on a glass plate in the centre. A gorgeous boy who was going out with a friend of mine turned up to pay his respects. 'Anna,' he said. 'I haven't brought presents and I haven't brought flowers, but I've got a lot of love if you need it.' I laughed and asked for a present instead.

It was now, sitting with people my age, picking seaweed out of a plate of hors-d'oeuvres, now that the funeral and the memorial service were over, now that the life insurance he'd never had but that the *Correspondent* had rustled up had been paid into my account, now that the mourners had dispersed to their corners of the world, to their lives, now I had really lost him for ever. No other business.

The next day there was a piece in one of the papers by someone who had been at the service. They had overheard a conversation between two of the guests. 'You have to have died young and tragically to have had a service like this,' one said to the other. The second replied, 'No you don't. You have to have been David Blundy.'

And that was exactly what I couldn't be, but I tried. I flew flailingly around, hoping that adventures and affairs might do the trick as they did (or didn't do) for him. Russia seemed to be the place furthest from anything familiar, but it only served to prove that the whole world was empty without Dad and his stupid smirking face.

Moscow, 1991

I was lying in the dark on an iron bed almost a year after that service. Everything outside was muffled by thick and still falling snow, and inside I could hear the rats trying to gnaw through the walls, through the old iron drainage grates and through the crumbling parquet floor. I had come home from work earlier, raw and red with cold, snow melting on the black fur of my coat and hat, to find a rat, dead in the bath. My Russian boyfriend, Sergei and I had tried to kill the rats with poison that I had brought back with me from England. Most of them ignored it, but the ones that succumbed in desperate hunger went mad with thirst and died trying to get to some water.

The old woman was murmuring audibly to herself in her sleep. She hadn't left the apartment for fifteen years and would pace up and down the dark corridor, dragging her festering foot behind her, babbling and laughing. She wore a quilted dressing gown that had once been pink and she let the pigeons into her room from the dark alleyway onto which our windows looked out. 'Annushka! Annushka!' she would call, toothlessly. If I felt brave enough I crept out of my room and let her beg cigarettes from me, or I might even look at the bowl of rotting potatoes she held out to me – all growths and tubules.

Once a week a boy called Lyosha would appear at our tall, painted door and I would remove the iron bar that secured it. 'It's me! Lyosha!' he called, and I made him describe me to me before I would open the door. 'You're Anna. You've got blonde hair,' he told me. He handed over a pink of milk, some potatoes and occasionally some cabbage, sausage or eggs. They were for the old woman. Every other week or so he would come just to apologise for the fact that there were no provisions to bring. In 1990 old people were starving to death all over Moscow.

I had had a lot to drink that night. Sergei and I had driven through the snow to a taxi park outside of town, skidding all over the place, getting out every now and then to wipe the windscreen. We saw a woman lying face down in the middle of the road in the black slush, still clutching her umbrella. The car that had hit her sat empty and crushed by her side, spilling petrol into the ice. 'This is a God-forsaken place, Toad,' murmured Sergei, drawing in his smoke and taking my hand over the gearstick.

The taxi parks were dangerous and I had been instructed to take out my earrings and not to speak in any circumstances. I hunched down inside the car, making ice patches in my scarf with my breath. Here you could buy alcohol, drugs, guns, women and all the German food aid that had been brought in by various charities to feed the elderly – packets of stuff to which you had to add unobtainable eggs, milk, cheese, meat or whatever. Not that anyone could read the instructions anyhow. The only good thing about the food aid was the cornflakes – Moscow's black market wealthy were flooded with German cornflakes for a couple of months.

This was a wasteland. It looked as though the area amid the high rise blocks had been cleared for construction, but at the moment it was just snow and cars parked in the pitch dark under the dim glow of the surrounding flats. It was so quiet you would hardly know there were people there, skulking in the cars. Occasionally you could see the orange fuzz of a cigarette in a window, or the flare of a match that someone was using to give his customer a glance at the goods. A lot of murders happened out here, but not many people considered these types to be any great loss.

Sergei stayed in the car and wound the window down an inch. 'Vodka. A litre,' he said to the shadow who approached, and held out 30 roubles. The notes were snatched from his hand and the man disappeared. I stared out at the blackness and Sergei smoked. When he believed it he would say to me, 'It's OK, Toad. Everything's going to be all right.' This time he was reserving judgement. Our way was blocked by two hulking men whose faces it was too dark to see. The shadow re-emerged and Sergei opened the window a fraction more for a bottle to be pushed through the gap. The bullish men moved out of the way and we drove off towards the street lights and the dancing snowflakes. The sticky bottle was in my lap and the taxi park was behind us.

At home we sat on the dirty parquet floor, either side of a candle that would explode when the flame got to the protruding wax roses, and we drank the yellow, viscous liquid from two-kopeck glasses with orange stripes round the rim. If you clutch them too firmly they break. It was certainly petrol mixed with something. 'You should take it back and complain,' I quipped across the flame. 'To your father,' said Sergei raising his glass. 'First anniversary, Dad!' I said, smiling ironically. It was 17 November 1990.

Now Sergei was asleep with one hand against the window ledge, and I was listening to the rats. My head was swimming and my heart was pounding. All the omens were coming true. The night I had said I was afraid of fires in these buildings I woke up to find our bed ablaze, the room light with flames and the corridor filled with smoke. Sergei dragged the mattress into the bathroom, and we stood there naked, laughing with fear, looking at it smoulder and sizzle. Watches wouldn't work on my wrist and disaster struck anyone I stood near. I saw old ladies fall on the ice, drunks walk under cars, train station gangsters pull knives on their rivals.

Sergei had called me 'Annushka who spilt the cooking oil' since we had met in 1985 because of Anna in Bulgakov's *The Master and Margarita*. She spills cooking oil on some tram lines and a character called Berlioz trips and is beheaded by the oncoming vehicle. I went into a super-market and smashed a bottle of cooking oil on the floor. 'Toad, that is not good,' said Sergei when I told him, laughing.

The next morning I awoke, so hungover I thought I might die, to see Sergei hopping across the cold wooden floor to answer the phone in the hall. It was an old, heavy, black phone with a stiff, rusting dial and sharp edges. Sergei was lighting a cigarette with one hand and had his other down his Y-fronts. I crawled out of bed in my orange silk pyjama top and padded to the kitchen for some hard-currency orange squash. My eyes hurt and my head swam and I had trodden on a dead cockroach. The old lady had left some gruel on the stove in a black iron pan. It had congealed. I retched.

When I clambered back over Sergei to get into bed he was staring blankly. 'My dad died. He had a brain haemorrhage.'

My friends in Moscow thought I was a witch. Everything had completely fallen apart without Dad and I had no idea what to do with myself but drink. So I drank.

My heart was beating so fast one night I stopped being able to breathe. I was gasping and holding on to the edge of the bed, no longer able to hear anything except my blood. 'Seriozha!' I yelped. 'Seriozha!' He woke up and leapt to the light switch. I was sitting up on my knees in a long white nightgown shaking and crying. The bare bulb illuminated the huge green stains on the ceiling, the yellow wallpaper coming away at the edges, the bowls of cigarette butts and the empty bottle of vodka rolling on the floor by the bed.

'Come on!' he said, pulling on his trousers. 'Get up.'

He sat me on the edge of the bed and put thick socks on my feet. He led me into the hall and made me put my boots, coat and scarf on over my nightie. I was still gasping for breath and clutching my chest. The corridor stank of cats and cabbage and there was a drunk lying on the floor at the bottom of the steps where the man with the wooden arm usually stood and swept.

The hem of my nightie was immediately wet from the snow and it stuck to my legs as I sat in the car. This Lada Samara took ten minutes to warm up. Sergei scraped the windscreen clean and dug us out with his shovel. The engine roared into the night.

In shivering silence we drove up to Lenin Hills. At times like this we always drove up to Lenin Hills. When we arrived I huddled under his grandfather's black trench coat and he walked me to the edge. There is a little church on the left and straight ahead lies the whole of Moscow – Kremlin domes twinkling, river white and solid in front of us and the suburbs creeping towards the horizon. 'I can't do it,' I said, steadier now. 'I can't do it without Dad.'

Sergei lit a cigarette and put it between my lips.

Pregnant and alcoholic, I eventually went back to England to have an abortion.

Letter of condolence from my Aunt Pauline, Dad's sister, November 1989
In our society we try and cover up our grief and really don't go through the grieving process. I have found out in the past, that it eventually catches up with one. Just when people think you should be back to normal and everything in perspective, one is crying over the slightest thing. I will miss David.

It was bad, but it had been worse and got worse again. I think now that every time I went away I was just trying not to go to El Salvador. I must have known even then that going might help me to recover, and I probably felt that recovery might mean forgetting, so I preferred to wallow. The summer after Dad was killed I went to China and took the train from Beijing to Moscow. China had been a respite from grieving and I had become fairly optimistic that I might be able to cope. I had travelled with a boyfriend from university and we had a blissful time, pottering around the country pretending to be an elderly couple from Skipton. But he had to fly back to Hong Kong and I got on the Trans-Siberian alone in a thin summer dress with a big rucksack on my back.

I met Edward on the first evening as the train trundled into the warm darkness towards Mongolia. Out in the corridor, isolated to the point of near insanity, I asked him for a light. He had long blond hair in a ponytail and big flip-flops on his feet. He was, it turned out, in his year off between school and university and would be going up to Oxford in October to read Russian and Latin. At least, he had a place but he might not be taking it because he wanted to commit suicide. He said this with complete seriousness, looking straight into my eyes through the dark and blowing his smoke out in a long stream. I laughed.

'How romantic!' I said. 'A pathetic gesture in the face of mortality. It's not long before someone takes it out of your hands.'

He nodded, uninterested in my derision, clear in his own intent. He meant it. For six days, as Siberia swept past in the sunlight and forests closed in in the night, as the Urals came and went and sunflower seeds were sold on the platform in Novosibirsk we talked about death. I sat on the cold metal floor in piles of cigarette ash and in the sticky mess our Coolaid orange powder and vodka cocktails had made and I insisted on life.

We hardly slept and we never stopped talking. If one of us went to the loo the other followed, stood outside the door and shouted. 'But why does the fact that there's no God, mean that . . .' My summer dresses got filthy, my hair was thick with grease, the train had no food once we crossed the border into Russia and we had become thin and shaking with the drink and the insomnia.

I talked about my dad. I talked about the things he had said and the way he had said them. I did imitations of him and as the train rattled through the night I sang Edward all the sad pop songs that reminded me of him. Dad was my main, my only argument for life. People like that exist. It's worth it.

Then one day we were sitting in the restaurant car

chewing stale black bread and drinking strong tea with
sugar in it and I looked at Edward's face. Suddenly the
futility of everything – the random bleak hell of the world
– swept over me. Silver birches flashed outside the window and they seemed thin compensation for all the
misery. The pointlessness was all-encompassing and I ran
back to my compartment, jumping hysterically over the
gaps between the carriages, slamming the heavy metal
doors, and shoving people out of the way. I told Edward
I would commit suicide with him.

Sergei met the two of us at the station in Moscow (we
had become inseparable) and took us to a café in a hotel.
I couldn't stop shaking. 'You are arrogant to assume so
much,' Sergei said when he had listened to my newly
formed opinions. 'That is what we know of the universe,'
he seethed, slapping his cigarette packet down into the
middle of the white plastic cloth. 'And this,' he said, drawing a large circle around it with his finger, 'is what we
don't know.'

Desperate for any kind of consolation, this tiny piece of
nothing relaxed me, and the sight of the churches he
showed us afterwards, the sunny Moscow courtyards,
dogs being walked and the air filled with *pukh* (dandelion
seeds and thistledown) seemed reason enough to me to go
on for now.

But every time I tried to fill the hole that Dad had left
with some new theory, some pseudo-religious drivel,
some new man, it seemed to get deeper and wider and
more all-engulfing. For the first few years I talked about
him to everyone. I went on dates and burst into tears in
expensive restaurants, eliciting a great deal of sexual desire

in the men on the other side of the table, for some reason. I was, I suppose, promiscuous and would sleep with anyone pretty who was willing to put their arms round me and listen to my angst and my stories about Dad.

Then I began to despise people who fell for damsels in distress and to despise myself for being one. 'Were you upset when your dad died?' they would ask over brandy. 'Could say that,' I might now snap before changing the subject. I stopped going out with boyish men who cared and didn't mind how much I cried, and started demanding my men be more like my father – glamorous, brave, exciting, funny. They failed and I hated them for it.

When I was singing in a band in Moscow in 1992 I met an American journalist who had a poem about artichokes on his kitchen wall and some empty shell casings on his bookcase. He owned all those fat political hardbacks that foreign correspondents have to have, he smoked carelessly and he seemed to like me.

We ate Chinese food and he asked if I would feel comfortable coming back to his place. He took my cigarette from my fingers and stubbed it out, lifted my glass of red wine from my hands and put it on the table, walked across the black and white lino, knelt by my chrome and leather stool and kissed me. We laughed, had sex and smoked Lucky Strikes until the pale Moscow dawn seeped through his bedroom blinds.

I mentioned that my dad had been killed, but I was past the stage when I would have tried to conjure up my father to demonstrate the extent of my loss. I think Brad mistook my reticence on the subject for sanity. I think he imagined I had come to terms with it, learnt to get on with my life, *got over* it. One thing you never do, as anyone bereaved knows, is get over it. Incorporate it into your life. Adapt your personality accordingly. Never be the same again. Yup. Get over it, no.

Brad and I went to dinner parties, dachas and restaurants. The snow thawed and we had drinks on the balconies. He said he loved me. I said I loved him. We lied. I thought I ought to love him because he was sane and paternal, stable and measured.

I even moved to Washington, DC to be with him, which was a big mistake. I hadn't been to Washington since Dad died. My Aunt Pauline had been to his flat ('that nasty, barren little condominium up poofs' alley that passes for home') near Dupont Circle, rifled through his tall suits and overflowing medicine cabinet. She had seen the dead trees on the balcony and the ball of crumpled washing still in the machine. She took their father's truncheon down off the wall and picked out some shirts that must still have smelt of Dad to bring over to me in England. It was Pauline who glanced up as she sorted, expecting Dad to leap round the corner and ask her what she thought she was doing, who must have thought she heard his key in the lock, his sigh as he dumped his bags down, flicked through his mail, threw his keys, passport and cigarettes on to the table.

Brad couldn't meet me when I flew into Dulles airport to come and live with him, but it didn't make any difference. If he had done he wouldn't have been Dad. As I stood outside in the sun waiting in line for a taxi, I looked over to where Dad's Mercedes had been in the car park the last time I had been here. I saw him lolloping towards me, hands in pockets, smirking.

I saw Dad in every restaurant Brad and I went to (I had

been to almost all of them before), on every street corner
and in the next aisle of every supermarket. I pointed out
places of significance to Brad and he nodded, but had no
interest. I hated Washington and I derided it at every turn.
I expected Brad, like Dad, to be my ally in this, but Brad
wasn't irreverent. He believed in democracy and the con-
stitution. He was proud of the President and the freedom
of the press. He had liked me for my disrespect for author-
ity, directly inherited from my father, and now he began
to hate me for it.

I found his self-seriousness and the way he actually
thought *Time* magazine was a worthy publication ridiculous and I was embarrassed by the way he was defined by
his job. I hated him for not being my father, for not telling
jokes to cheer me up, for not introducing me to funny
people and for not being my ally against the world.

Washington, DC, 1988
Dear Slime Bucket,

Who are you? Why do I keep getting these nasty
little scrawled notes on both sides of lined paper? My
friends in the Washington DC First Precinct are now
intercepting my mail and throwing away the nasty
scrawled notes. Most of my letters, and the postman
arrives groaning with mail each morning, are now on
cards with embossed gold lettering. I presume you
have read and probably memorised the illuminating
piece I wrote on the police and the murder rate in
Washington in the *Sunday Telegraph* magazine (God
rot it) – the murder rate is awful and Washington is
now Murder City, USA, according to the *Washington
Post*. Most people I know have been murdered. Poor

Ben [Macintyre] got his the other night and Patrick
Cockburn is in the intensive care unit of the George
Washington Memorial Hospital recovering from
multiple stab wounds. He had almost recovered from
the stabbing when someone rushed into his room and
shot him. According to the statistics (this bit is true) if
the murder rate continues to rise at this level everyone
will have been murdered by 1994. Why not come
over in April?

Went out with the police for three nights. The best
bit was when a police car I was in arrested three
members of the urban under class (black as night) who
were driving along innocently in a very smart car.
The policeman I was with, nice officer Smythe,
assumed, correctly, that they had stolen it, turned his
siren on and went in hot pursuit. He radioed in
another eight cars who cornered them somewhere in
South East Washington. The driver made a run for it
– an obvious confession of guilt – and we cornered
him by ramming him up against a wire fence with the
front of Officer Smythe's car. Officer Smythe then
asked me to put my foot on the drug crazed, car
stealing fiend, who was spread eagled on the floor,
while he found his handcuffs which he had left in the
car. I did so with alacrity and entered into the spirit of
the whole thing. 'One move or even breath out of
you, scum bag, and you're history,' I hissed. He
trembled. His eyes flickered so I said: 'Don't even
think of it, you pool of rat's wee-wee, or you're
going to have one leg shorter than the other, so
freeze, creepoid features,' I muttered under my
breath. He lay pretty still I can tell you.

Unfortunately I have the feeling that he was completely innocent. The car had been stolen about a year ago, but he said he bought it three months ago from a friend in Anacostia. When nice officer Smythe asked why he had run away he said, quite reasonably in my opinion, 'Because you mother-fuckers were chasing after me.' He will probably be executed if not for stealing a car then for use of foul language.

I hated me for not being my father too. I hated everything.

Brad and I were eating oysters in a Georgetown restaurant where I had been with Dad and Samira and where the waitress mistook me for Drew Barrymore and I burst into tears. I couldn't stop crying. I was lonely and drunk and had nobody to laugh with.

And that was one of my better post-Dad relationships.

I soon moved back to England. But I found that here, so much more than abroad, I consistently failed to compete adequately with Dad's memory. Journalists especially, I thought, expected me to be like him and I wasn't a good enough replacement by any stretch of the imagination.

When Dad left the *Sunday Times* he wrote his colleagues a note which ended:

I know that I have left it [the Middle East] in more slender and probably more competent hands than my own. Colvin is good, but you don't have to use words like 'stunning' and 'gosh' when you read her copy from Libya (much of it culled from a piece of my own as I remember). I wish you all the best, even Colvin

who is taking over my job, my flat, my car, my
computer, my new crystal glasses and is about to enter
into a meaningful relationship with Samira.

My warmest regards,

David.

This was Marie Colvin of the *Sunday Times*. I started at
the *Sunday Times* in 1994 and met her there. It was an
entirely ghastly experience apart from the fact that Marie,
and a few other great people (Rebecca Fowler, Leslie
Thomas, Julie Cohen, Simon Reeve and Janine di
Giovanni, all of whom have now left) were languishing
there too. Marie is clever and beautiful and sexy and
everything you would hope a Middle East correspondent
would be. She wore amazingly short skirts, displaying her
amazingly long legs, always seemed mildly hungover and
kept lots of glamorous young men in tow. She was nice to
me because I was David's daughter. She wrote me lewd
messages in the computer system and we went out on a
double date. I went round to her house in Notting Hill
first and she poured me a colossal neat vodka and talked
about Dad. Over dinner she charmed both our dates fairly
conclusively and I went home early, leaving them at a
murky club called Green Street being insalubrious.

This, of course, was before she fell in love with Juan
Carlos – a huge Bolivian war correspondent whom Dad
had mistaken for a guerrilla on first meeting him. He had
said something like, 'Excuse me, are those the enemy
lines?' in rubbish Spanish. Juan Carlos had said something
like, 'How the fuck should I know?' in perfect English.
He used to call Marie up at the office and shout, 'Hurry
up and find her! I'm the King of Spain!' They were each

the only person in the world who wouldn't be completely crushed by the other's force of personality. Perfect.

But their wedding was no fun at all. I mean, I'm sure it was wonderful for them – they danced merengue and there was loads to drink, all their friends were there from all over the world and everything went according to plan. I, however, was absolutely miserable. Here they were. Every single one of Dad's friends in one room. All the people whose names I had been forced to memorise throughout my childhood. All the people who had been at his funeral and memorial service. And they were having a fantastic time without him. I wanted someone to stop me and say something poignant about Dad.

Letter of condolence from Allen Pizzey of CBS, November 1989
My lasting memory of David is of a gangling figure in a cracked leather jacket, hair ruffled, slightly bemused tone, and concern for others, and what was right, above all else. It has been said, and will oft be repeated, that David was a good friend, a fine colleague, and a great reporter. When you hear and read such things, believe them, for they are true, and in the world that was David's, there are no higher accolades.

I arrived quite late in a very short, bright green dress which had seemed quite a laugh when I put it on, but when I turned up alone in a room of my colleagues and my father's contemporaries it seemed ridiculous and provocative. The room was dark and seething, with high ceilings and loud Latin music thumping about the place.

People were eating platefuls of salmon and chicken and everyone looked to have slurped down a bev or two already.

Janine di Giovanni (also virtually naked) came over to talk to me, thank God, and was about the only person I spoke to that evening who was genuinely friendly, unintimidating and sweet. Her dress was black, shiny and very tight and she is extremely beautiful, but she was smiley and manages to speak without the hysterical ironic grimace which characterises the older British foreign correspondents. (Marie Colvin and Janine, I hasten to add, are American.)

Dad, I suppose, would have been one of these people by now. These older men, once at the edge of every battlefield, now desperately holding on to their jobs, freelancing from the places they loved best or traipsing into East London every day to fulfil some editorial post of the kind they spent their lives deriding, but for which they are now pathetically grateful. Their wives and girlfriends have left them, their wars are over, their drinking is alcoholism now, not *joie de vivre*, and their faces are withered, not rugged. I wouldn't have wished that on him, but then perhaps he would have been canny enough to escape it, like Ian Jack (editor of *Granta*) or Jon Connell (editor of the *Week*), among the few.

A knackered old drunk who is under the impression that having bullets flying past your ears for three decades is a sufficient substitution for intelligence and a personality came up to me to tell me that the weekly column I write for the *Times* Saturday magazine is crap. Yeah, well, OK. I would be the first to admit that if you put it next to anything my father ever wrote, or indeed any piece of investigative reporting that is half well written then, of course, my frivolous, voyeuristic column about my own tedious life is crap. If, however, you set it against other personal columns and your average piece of trash feature journalism, then it is bordering on adequate. Anyway, why on earth would an older man come and tell a young woman that what she does for a living is crap? It is an endless source of bafflement to me.

'Your father wouldn't approve,' he dribbled.

'I didn't approve of most things he did either,' I spat.

The drunk laughed mirthlessly. I asked him if he had children. I was wondering if he would have appreciated it if my father had talked to his daughter like this. He has no children. Suddenly, from across the room the man I was seeing at the time approached. I was elated and fell into his arms.

'I'm in a really bad mood,' he said and I sank. If ever I had needed a little ray of sunshine to sparkle into my life it was this evening.

Still, he did perform the key task of being fantastically rude to the editor of the *Sunday Times* for me. Said editor was standing alone, shyly clutching his glass of wine. Said boyfriend went and baited him for a while. 'I'm sure I know you. Aren't you in the media or something?' he asked him. 'I'm the editor of the *Sunday Times*,' said editor, flattered. 'No, no . . . I don't think that was it . . .' muttered boyfriend dismissively and wandered off for a drink. That was the high point of the evening.

I had far too much wine and began to miss Dad painfully. I wanted to creep under someone's arm, be spoken for, have someone to introduce me to people so that they would have to be nice to me, find someone to take me home. I told a few of his friends that I found his absence upsetting. They were dismissive of this drunken girl whose journalism they despised and in whose bereavement they had lost interest seven years before. Well, perhaps they weren't, but I was feeling paranoid. My boyfriend was dancing with Siobhan Darrow, a spectacular CNN correspondent who knew Dad and is a very close friend of mine. She was in relationship hell herself so I didn't feel I could really ask her to keep her hands off my boyfriend, particularly as he was making it fairly clear that he was wanting to lay them on. I was too shy to dance at that stage of sobriety because I am a rubbish dancer, so I sulked energetically instead.

I met Siobhan Darrow in Moscow outside a meeting that the Russian and American foreign ministers were having. It was minus 27 and we were almost crying with the cold. I had picked up a tripod for one of the cameramen and stupidly stuck my hand to it, so I was stamping about in pain. It was a very clear night with millions of bright stars, and Moscow was exciting and on the change. It was 1992. Shiv was there for CNN, I, in a menial capacity, for ABC News. I sloped around the office doing photocopies, answering the phone and being in love with the correspondent.

He took me out to dinner and said, 'You're an original, Anna Blundy.' I ate lobster and tried to stop myself proposing to him. I failed. He was flattered to be paid this attention by a girl whose father and his clique of whisky-drinking, leather-jacketed cronies had written him off as a red-faced dweeb. He had know Dad when he began as a television correspondent, covering the Middle East. He had, I inferred, been in awe of the more macho print journalists who monopolised the bar and had glamorous girlfriends. I doubt that he had really been excluded from Dad's circle (into which, it seemed to me, any old drunk was welcome) but he is desperately shy so he probably excluded himself.

'God, you remind me of your father,' Shiv said that first night we met, sending billows of white breath into the night and raising one eyebrow in disconcertion. She couldn't believe that this man who seemed so young could have a daughter this old. She couldn't believe that this man, who was dead, could have so effectively replicated himself in female form. I had this effect on a lot of people who knew Dad.

So Siobhan and my boyfriend were swaying and beaming at each other and I kept going off to the loo to check my make-up and my hair. I felt grotesque and out of place. Boyfriend had little interest in my entirely unengaging condition and sauntered away to talk to Ben Okri, with whose presence he was fantastically impressed. 'I'm having a really good time,' he kept telling me as I was on the verge of tears. My shoes were too high. I was making a spectacle of myself.

It was by far my worst 'competing with Dad' evening. His shoes were wandering listlessly and emptily around the room and I couldn't fill them. I had spent years turning into him in terms of emotional instability and crippling angst, but I couldn't do it in terms of wit, charm, intelligence and professional prowess.

For a while after he died I used to love being with Dad's friends and being told I looked like him, reminded them of him, had inherited his sense of humour. I loved it when my mum said, 'You're just like Dave,' when I loped off a plane in his leather jacket and a pair of ridiculous trainers. But then, as my career as a semi-serious journalist was ended by the *Sunday Times*, and as my relationships and prolonged depressions were plunging me into the ridiculous, I could only focus on the galling lack of similarities between myself and my father. He left without telling me what to do.

At Marie's wedding party I kept thinking to myself, as I disappointed yet another of his friends with my lack of charisma, Dad, I can't do it on my own! Come back and get me out of this! All I could do was wonder why he had liked some of these people. Then I remembered that he had never actually claimed to like most of them, so maybe he just spoke to them because not many other people would. I could imagine them muttering to each other, 'It's such a shame the way Anna Blundy's turned out. She looks terrible. I hear she's a slut.'

As I picked out my revelling boyfriend in the blurring whirl I caught sight of the bride and groom dancing together, smiling into each other's eyes. She was happy and gorgeous and he looked reassuring and sparkly-eyed. I realised that the problem was not with some of their more raddled guests, but with me. I was totally lost in this world without Dad to have the personality on behalf of us both.

Eventually I hit the falling over and sobbing stage and my boyfriend must have taken me home because I woke up in the morning to find him staring wildly into clouds of his own cigarette smoke next to me.

It was then, last year, that I realised I was going to have

to go and face it, go to Salvador, and meet the people who had seen it happen.

El Salvador, 1997

Mike Lanchin had agreed to meet me at the Camino Real. I had spoken to him over the telephone and heard a child's voice in the background. I knew he worked for the BBC and I was anticipating a very British family man, someone reassuring and homely. I didn't expect him to be wry and funny and North-London-ish. If I'd met him anywhere else I'd have guessed he was a solicitor, a barrister, or a doctor at the outside. His sister works for Channel 4. It was confusing to be presented with such a familiar figure in such unfamiliar surroundings. But Lanchin has been in El Salvador for ten of his thirty or so years, working for radio stations and marrying young women who fought for their cause. His wife is a decade younger than he is but, he says, twenty years is a long time in El Salvador, and he is right, of course.

He has short gingery hair, a short-sleeved shirt, a beaten-up car and a fastidious manner. I said I wanted a cup of coffee and he took me to a place in a mall called Mr Donut. It was air-conditioned and like any kind of drive-up place in America where you would pull over for coffee and a donut on your way to the Grand Canyon as part of your fly-drive holiday booked on Hendon High Street. The serving girls had little white paper hats on, name badges and brown uniforms. They smiled as they served us and pointed out the napkins, sugar and stirrers. It was weird. The heat and dust outside suddenly belonged somewhere else, and the fact that everyone was speaking Spanish was overlookable.

Lanchin tore the corner off his sachet of sugar and asked me about Dad. Who? What? Why? Where? When? Journo-questions, pouring out, no doubt, subconsciously. He had a list of suggestions – people I should call – and I wrote them down in my book. The coffee was watery and American and the rim of the cup too thick to drink out of.

We sat there, on these orange plastic seats, in strangely formal surroundings when out of nowhere they started piping. 'Wherever you are, whatever you do, I will be right here waiting for you. Whatever it takes, oh how my heart aches, I will be right here waiting for you,' into the ambience of Mr Donut, central San Salvador. For the first time since I'd got there I had an overwhelmed-with-grief moment.

I'd felt so capable, so brave, so facing-up-to-everything and efficient with my notebook, my pocketful of colones and my Spanish dictionary. Now I felt little-girlish and pathetic. I missed Dad. He'd have thought Mr Donut was hilarious and he would have been fascinated by Mike Lanchin. He liked incongruity and there was loads of it going down in Mr Donut that afternoon. My eyes filled with tears and I bit into my cinnamon ring.

'So, is it just the one child you have?' I asked, beaming.

I had nearly finished now. Salvador was beginning to seem basically familiar. I no longer expected to get shot at every crossroads and I was beginning to be able to differentiate between gang members and middle-class house-wives.

I set off for the archbishop's office. The heat was no longer bothering me so much and I had started noticing my hangovers which had been eclipsed before by the nov-

elty of all the available experiences. I had stopped noticing the guns and was beginning to see what Marvin had
meant on the plane on the way over – it was just like any
other city. It was in a way. It was possible to get money
out (just) and to buy clothes and food, to go to the cinema
and to bars and to have your car repaired if it broke down.
There was a commercial centre, amusement arcades, a red
light district and a cathedral.

I asked my taxi driver to go to the Archovispado on the
Calle San Jose and wait. 'Maria Julia Hernandez?' I said to
a hot-looking man slouching on some steps. He smiled
warmly and pointed inside. I clacked along some Soviet-
style corridors (closed doors, peeling cream-coloured
paint, fluorescent lighting and a smell of polish) until a
woman with huge hair peeped out of a room at the end.
She was tiny and smiling, with a Margaret Thatcher
hairdo and Queen Mother shoes. There was a portrait of
Archbishop Romero above her desk and lots of photos of
other dead priests dotted around the room. She had
worked for Romero before his assassination and had been
tirelessly dedicated to the cause of justice throughout the
conflict as her friends and colleagues were tortured and
killed.

Her belief in God and the ultimate goodness of
mankind seems, judging by the calm and gentleness of her
manner, not to have been shaken. As I walked into her
office she took both my hands in hers and looked straight
up into my face. 'I am so sorry about your father,' she said.
'He was a great man, but he was killed in the line of duty.
There is great honour in that.' I burst into tears.

This was the first woman I had spoken to since I had
arrived. The first person who had understood the nature

of my visit. The men all took me for an investigator of the circumstances. Maria Julia knew I had just come to see, to think about Dad and to lay some things to rest.

She didn't try to stop me crying or to distract me. She just smiled softly and carried on looking at me. Despite all the awful things she had seen and heard about she still understood that the loss of someone you love is terrible every time. The fact that it has happened to a lot of people in ways far more terrible doesn't help. She handed me a few photocopies, smooth, stacked and stapled together. There was a list of journalists who had been killed in the conflict and Dad's name was neatly highlighted. November 17th 1989 *periodista ingles*, David Michael Blundy. Eros's dad was in there too.

Then there were the reports from the local papers.

Diario Latino 17 de noviembre de 1989 — Herido periodista inglés
El periodista inglés David Michael Blundy, de 44 años, resulto herido hoy durante enfrentamientos armados en Mejicanos, siendo trasladado de urgencia al Hospital Rosales donde fue operado de emergencia.

'La Prensa Gráfica' 18 de noviembre de 1989
Muerte periodista británico mientras cubria combates

There were a few more similar accounts, some with photos of Dad, looking intense, impatient, intrepid. He didn't look, in any of the post-death pictures in the papers, as though he were just about to break into a smile. Odd, because that's actually how he looked all the time – mischievous and silly.

Snivelling, I left Maria Julia's office, thanking her over-keenly for her help, which was non-existent really in so far as the bits of paper and actual information were concerned. In the taxi I looked at the photographs and the Spanish headlines and was moved. Tiny little articles, from page four, page five and page twenty-seven. Probably not many people even read them. It can't have seemed to have mattered much at the time. But it mattered to me, I thought, straightening my white dress and glaring fiercely out at the street. It mattered to me.

'Donde?' asked the cab driver, pulling out into the roaring traffic.

'El Camino Real,' I replied, jutting my chin and stuffing the papers into my bag.

By now I had run out of money and was depending on the reluctant charity of my new friends. I had a job and was rich, they figured. They didn't and were poor. It was a case of Credomatic. Two days in a row I pulled up in the Credomatic courtyard, a secluded little venue not far from my hotel, on a street of middle-class, single-storey houses, white with bright hanging flowers.

Credomatic is heavily guarded and teenagers in uniforms wave their guns randomly around while they light their cigarettes and chat to each other. Eros and I had our cameras removed from us before entering air-conditioned first world heaven but they didn't check us for weapons. I had tried to wheedle money out of some fat girl with a perm but my bank in England refused the credit. I set my alarm for 4 a.m. and made a hysterical call to Martin at Barclays in Oxford, banging my mini-bar Perrier bottle on my Gideons bible for emphasis. The next day, glancing superciliously at my passport and clearly doubting its authenticity (this always makes me doubt it too), she handed over 1,500 colones. I have a few hundred colones in a box at home, the ones Dad would have used for his taxi to the airport or for tipping Romero at reception who remembered him from the war – 'A very good man.'

I then had to go to Tom Long's house to be briefed for our impending pilgrimage to Mejicanos. 'Al atrás del estadion Florblanca,' I told the driver who nodded vigorously. We trundled off round the block, screeching and beeping the horn, and pulled up outside a hefty little building with gunmen outside. The driver asked them where number 45 was and, despite the fact that it turned out to be next door, they said they didn't know. I didn't like having an AK47 poked in my eye as the guy leant into the front window, so I told the driver to pull off. As he did so the bloke with the black cap and firearms shouted, 'Gringo?' The driver braked. 'Si! Si!' I squealed at him. He pointed to a metal door in the next building. 'Gringo,' he confirmed and sauntered back to his post.

The gringo in question ('Fuck. A guy with a gun knows where I'm at,' he giggled) had just had a shower and his bare feet slapped on the stone floor as he walked away from the door with a towel round his waist. A cigarette hung out of his mouth and there was a bottle of beer on the table. Photographs he had taken of erupting volcanoes hung on the walls of the vast and gloomy L-shaped room.

Eros soon handsomed along and banged on the metal door. He slouched towards the table where he sat hunched and smoking, not in a good mood. He held his cigarette between his thumb and middle finger and blew lazy smoke rings that formed the blue haloes above his head.

'I was supposed to go to Mejicanos with those guys,' said Tom, rubbing his head with a towel and casually telling me things I had waited almost a decade to hear. 'I had been two days before and I'd tried to go in the front way but there was a sniper in the bell tower near the crossroads and he was firing at us, so we took a long detour round the back and got behind the rebel lines that way. I told your father and this guy Gasparini that, and we were going to meet in the lobby after curfew the morning of the 17th and go out there, but they didn't wait for me and they got a taxi with, I think, Gentile and Robles, and went in the front.' He waved a pencil around to show the locations.

I had seen a photograph of the crossroads, shown to me by Commander Tony Comben of Scotland Yard who investigated Dad's murder at the time for the coroner's report. He and his team had been brought in to find the murderers of the six Jesuits slaughtered on 16 November 1989. In Commander Comben's photographs the crossroads looked seedy and fairly nondescript, certainly not the scene of a battle or a death. Just a dirty, third world crossroads with a traffic light hanging from a wire across the street. The taxi drivers who served the journalists from the Camino Real at that time were reluctant to go to Mejicanos that day and they pulled round the corner from the deadly intersection, in effect exposing their fares to fire. Bill Gentile, a *Newsweek* photographer who shared Dad's cab on the morning of 17 November, was the one who says he believes Dad may have been mistaken for a guerrilla because of his blue shirt. Tom Long and the local

Salvadoreans don't think that possible. Everyone knew the press arrived in taxis, the taxis tended to have white handkerchiefs wrapped around their aerials and the journalists carried notebooks and cameras and were for the most part gringos. They would have been easily identifiable.

I suppose it was that apartness from the battle, the fact that the hacks were unmistakable, men and women on a worthy mission, that must have made them feel so immune to the dangers.

In the years after Dad died, I always felt that if I could just go to all these places where he had been and turn myself into the other one – not the one left at home and waiting – then perhaps everything might be all right. I might become immune to sadness. I kept on and on hopelessly trying it. I went to cities he had spent lots of time in and hopelessly sought him out.

Cairo, 1994

I arrived alone, late at night off the BA flight. The taxi sped past wailing mosques, flickering neon signs, endless balconies billowing with washing, buildings and flyovers piled one on top of the other, people spilling out of everywhere and traffic screaming into the hot night. The driver fiddled with his prayer beads and tapped his fingers on the dashboard to the whining of his tinny stereo.

There was no war to cover and no explosive situation to monitor, but I could nonetheless understand the addiction to the thrill of arriving alone, somewhere hot and totally alien, into a situation that is completely unpredictable. Everything you have left behind in England dwindles into nothingness as the sand seeps into your shoes and blows through your hair.

I phoned Mark Nicholson of the *FT* and announced myself to him as soon as I had arrived at my hotel. 'I'll just finish up here and then why don't you come over to my place and we can drink gin and tonics on the balcony and watch the sun go down over the Nile?' he said. The Nile. I had only ever sung about the Nile (when I was the narrator in *Joseph and the Amazing Technicolor Dreamcoat* at school) or watched Agatha Christie films set on it. This was easily the most romantic invitation I had received in my life.

The gin and tonics were perfect, the sunset orange, pink and red and the balcony seemed to swoop out over the palms to the river where feluccas bobbed precariously in the swell. We went out for dinner at the Nile Hilton and I was, as ever, sitting next to a woman who had known my father in Lebanon. (She cried.) Mark and I then took a 2 a.m. horse and carriage ride through the chaos of Cairo's streets.

On that trip I worked with a photographer called Norbert Schiller (another of these heat-crazed hacks with wild eyes and a death-wish) and we sat for hours on the terrace of the Nile Hilton smoking shisha pipes and drinking beer. A toothless man in white robes would stagger through the heat haze to change out coals and exchange obscenities in Arabic with Norbert. I was the only woman on the terrace and Norbert was usually the only western man. The foreigners tend to keep to the inside of the hotel, while the locals come out to smoke. There was something reassuring about the way Norbert wore a leather jacket in the sun, never shaved, hitched his camera bag up on to his shoulder and glanced impatiently around. He made me feel at home.

Within four days of being in Egypt I had fallen in love with another journalist, whose identity I will make a cursory effort to protect. We walked in the desert together and looked at the horses. He shooed the child beggars away from us around the dusky Pyramids by making them laugh rather than insulting and frightening them. I don't know what he said. He took me for dinner at the Mena House Hotel and we ate curry and talked about our oddly similar upbringings. Then we went and drank gin on a floating bar on the Nile where the writer Mahfouz goes and we drove round the palm groves and saw a band of shabby boys washing their horses in the stream, robes hitched up round their waists.

'Where do you want to go now?' he asked.

'Somewhere we can drink, be outside and see the Nile,' I said.

'My house?' he offered.

I laughed and refused. I still regret it. He left me a note at my hotel the next day saying he regretted it too, but I didn't see him again.

So I had drunk at the bars Dad had been to, I had met lots of people who knew and liked him and had done all the things, surely, that he had done in Cairo. But it still felt empty. I didn't feel any closer to him at all. Further away, if anything. I understood the late-night phone calls now, I knew how lonely it was in a random hotel room, I could see the allure of people you would never know better than you did that night and I had fallen in love with the Middle East. I had read his postcards and received the presents and now, defiant, I was here myself, buying my own presents and sending my own postcards, but it didn't work.

Washington, DC, 1988

Alexandria is one of the most God forsaken rat holes in the history of the world. I went there once for lunch, a piece of half cooked camel's winkle with a stoat's eyeball for desert. The food had a horrible smell but luckily you didn't notice for the smell of old A-rab's armpit and camel dung pouring in through the window. I'd read that over-written, cliché-ridden nonsense by Lawrence Durrell – *The Alexandria Quartet* – which is just one big festering lie from beginning to end. Alexandria is like Ponders End in a heat wave with lots of people wearing bits of old cloth on their heads and vowing to murder that nice Salman Rushdie.

I never made it to Alexandria but I wrote some pieces from Cairo and none of them compared with Dad's. Even today when I file copy by phone to *The Times*, the copy-takers often say:, 'Ah, you must be the daughter of the great David Blundy,' and then I am ashamed to go on and read my silliness to them.

I made a point of never reading a single word the man wrote in life, so after his death I was surprised by and resentful of Dad's fantastic ability to capture things succinctly and without sentimentality. I am sure he would appreciate my resentment on this issue as I appreciated his on my Oxford entrance and on passing my driving test first time.

The 'Sunday Times' Magazine, 10 August 1986

Batn El Bakara ('the stomach of the cow') must be a strong contender for the title of the most unpleasant place to live on earth. It lies at the bottom of a valley carved into a mountain of Cairo's garbage. There are hills of compacted refuse rising on either side, smoking as it rots and ferments in the sun, and the houses are constructed of garbage, corrugated iron sheeting, boxes, cartons and pieces of plastic. At one end of the village is a fetid lake half full of rubbish.

Between 1,200 and 1,300 people live in Batn El Bakara. They are all Muslims. Other colonies of Coptic Christian garbage-collectors live in other parts of the vast dump. The inhabitants collect the rubbish from the streets of Cairo on carts pulled by donkeys and bring it back to the village where whole families, including the youngest children, sort through stinking heaps of it by hand. Among other horrors, they will pick through a carpet of flies to strip the rotting flesh from pieces of fish so that the bones can be sold to the factory up the road.

The temperature deep in the rubbish reaches over 40 degrees C, and there is no breeze. The air is strong. Flies form a thin haze and cover everything. A small boy lies on a bed, his nose, mouth and eyes covered so thickly by flies that he seems dead. He is fine, says his mother. Just sleeping.

I took Dad's word for this phenomenon.

But it was Beirut, where he eventually met Samira, that had all the time been the truly menacing place, the city where I had always assumed Dad would die. He would sometimes call me from the Commodore Hotel in the middle of the night and hold the phone out of the window so I could listen to the war. He made tapes of the noise on his Dictaphone and would play them when he burst into the bathroom to bomb my bath with pumice stones, bottles of shampoo and bars of soap. For years I watched the news expecting it to carry a story about his kidnap and murder.

I had always hated the news when I was little because Dad watched and listened to it so often and so intently. I thought it was boring and distracted attention from where it rightly belonged – with me. Now I was gripped by it, forced to listen carefully in case it took my father away for good.

They took Dad's friend Charlie Glass, whose house in London I had recently eaten barbecue at. Dad always said he knew where he was being held, somewhere in the Bekaa Valley I think he said, but that there was nothing anyone could seriously do about it without getting Charlie killed in the attempt. As it happened, he escaped by himself. Foreigners were flooding out of Beirut and Dad, of course, was flooding in. He was, I was pretty sure, doing this just to spite me. This was where the danger, the excitement, the women, the edge, the real life was. Dicey but worth the risk. London was where the soul dies. I was stuck in London feeling as drab as I looked. Thirteen, and hardly a green-eyed Lebanese temptress with contacts in the Druzes.

Not any more! In 1996 I went to Beirut. I went on a lavish press trip with British Mediterranean Airlines and I was in the unexpectedly glamorous company of Alan Whicker, Bruce Anderson and Lady Carla Powell. We stayed at the Al Bustan Hotel up in the hills around the city where the rich people hang out, and we could see Beirut sparkling and glimmering below as only Middle

Eastern cities do. I think it is something to do with the electricity. As you walk in the door of the hotel men with huge moustaches and Ali Baba trousers serve you thimblefuls of spicy coffee from an elaborate brass pot, and fleets of shining Mercedes stand outside the entrance waiting to whisk the wealthy to their destinations of choice. I made friends with a flamboyantly camp man called Robert Tewdr Moss who wore velvet cravats and made lewd comments about the shisha pipes brought to our table. It was like being in the Lebanon with Kenneth Williams. 'Ooooh! Suck on that, dear,' he oozed. Robert and I found all the same waiters attractive ('Look at that one in the fez!') and spent the four days gleefully drooling.

We took a cab down into the town on a cool night when fog was licking in and out of the black wounds in the devastated buildings. Big chunks were missing out of everything and the remaining walls were peppered with bullet holes – scars of murders and their attempts. The Ferris wheel that survived the war was silhouetted against the fog on the Corniche and the Hilton and Holiday Inn where so much of the fighting had taken place stood empty, still and ghastly in the night. The St Georges on the seafront, once glitteringly fashionable, not allowing the young photographer Don McCullin in without a tie, was a dark abandoned carcass by the building site which will be the new commercial district.

The silence and desolation, the obvious faded grandeur, were a more fitting monument than Cairo to Dad's absence. Life here hadn't gone on. The fighting had stopped, the dangerous green line separating East and West Beirut had been forgotten – cross at your leisure – and the Commodore Hotel where the press pack had swarmed was boarded up and empty. I was dying to tell Dad I was here, hanging out at a juice bar, sauntering idly down a street where once I would have been sniped at. I wanted him there to show me what had been where, who had been funny or brave or stupid. I stood in the dark outside the empty Commodore and said goodbye. Shut out as usual. No change there.

Robert and I strolled down the Corniche, caught by the spray of the crashing waves. We found a love letter and some money that someone had dropped and Robert read it out, translating from the running ink in the taxi on the way back.

In fact that night in the fog was deceptive. The Commodore was actually closed because it has been completely rebuilt and was awaiting a grand reopening. The St Georges and its yacht club are already, I think, back in business. The Ferris wheel is spinning again, rebuilding of the commercial sector has begun and even in the ruined buildings life is going on, people are beginning again. Personally, though, I will remember it as Robert and I saw it.

Robert was murdered six months later in his flat in London. The last time I spoke to him he was writing a piece about psychics. 'My darling,' he exclaimed. 'I've been sucked into the *demi-monde!*'

The 'Sunday Times' Magazine, 22 September 1985
Normal life in the city has a surreal tinge to it, which becomes almost addictive to the foreigners who choose to live there. At a cocktail party for an Australian teacher in a flat overlooking the Corniche, we watched glowing red tracer bullets from a heavy

machine gun somewhere behind us in the city bouncing like flat stones off the sea until they fizzled out.

Liz Sly, who is English and has lived in Beirut for three years, says that conversations at Beirut parties turn sometimes into a macabre Monty Python sketch. One person will say: 'A shell hit my apartment building last week.' 'That's nothing,' another guest will say. 'My dining room was wrecked by a rocket-propelled grenade.' 'You're lucky,' says another, 'I was kidnapped, locked in the boot of a car, blindfolded and interrogated for three days.' A nurse was chatted up in the lobby of a hotel by a bearded man who boasted that he was one of the hijackers of the TWA jet in June. She declined his overtures; but there is evidence that he is indeed one of the original hijackers, wandering freely in West Beirut and boasting of his exploits.

Outside the Commodore Hotel in West Beirut, where most of the foreign journalists stay, two militias, one Druze and one Shiite, confronted each other and fought for two or three hours with rifles, machine guns and rockets. Then, on Hamra, the two militia leaders approached each other and embraced. The little tiff was over. The bodies of three dead militiamen were carried off. The shops re-opened and life returned quickly to normal.

I find it galling that he was having such a good time while I worried about him. He would forever drone on about driving around in some armoured car listening to the Fine Young Cannibals and how it wasn't quite the same thing listening to 'She Drives Me Crazy' on your car stereo in London. It's not the horror of war that is addictive to war journalists. It is the lack of horror. All the nice things that suddenly seem so incongruous and so much nicer for the fact that they are surprising. Listening to your teenage daughter tell you about her exam results and how the dog is, while the hotel windows shatter around you.

Lewis Chester, the 'Sunday Correspondent', 21 November, 1990
Blundy's restlessness in terms of place and people was wholly genuine. 'He had the lowest threshold of boredom I have ever known,' says Tony Holden, a former *Sunday Times* colleague, 'and that meant a laugh every 35 seconds, or moving on.' David May, another *Sunday Times* writer, says, 'Where other people might worry about what they're going to do for the next year, Blundy would worry about the next minute.' It was a condition that could lead to some incredible feats of absent-mindedness.

May was with Blundy, 'missing, presumed dead', for four days in 1978, when the Israelis overran their apartment block just outside Tyre in Southern Lebanon. 'I remember waking up in the middle of the night and the Israelis were blitzing over our heads. Blundy had this huge flashlight on. We were right at the top of the block so it could be seen for miles around.' I said. "Christ, Blundy, what are we doing, trying our best to get killed?" He said, "Oh sorry, Dave, but I just can't find my bloody matches."'

Chapter Nine

My own dim life should teach me this,
That life shall live for evermore,
Else earth is darkness at the core,
And dust and ashes all that is;

19th April 1997

It was National Secretaries' Day in El Salvador. Becoming a secretary is something clearly hankered after by all Salvadorean women. Confectioners sell chocolate telephones and typewriters for people to give to their girlfriends, wives and daughters when the great day arrives. They do chocolate guns with chocolate bullets for the men.

Anyway, Secretaries' Day meant that the glorious Camino Real was swarming with young women in brightly coloured skirt suits and thick, garish make-up. They all wore high heels and walked with a lazy wiggle. They seemed elated and flirtatious, piling their plates up at the poolside buffet and tapping their feet under the tables to the band. A stage had been erected by the blue water and a 200-piece ensemble, all wearing black, was performing salsa and merengue numbers at incredible volume. The speakers were as tall as the stage canopy on both sides. There was a bloke with maracas, six saxophonists, a long line of backing singers with tambourines who did simple dance steps when they weren't involved in the song, then all the usual stuff and a female singer in a beige suit and high heels who kept her Sue Ellen glasses on throughout the set. It was 100 degrees in the shade and they were all sweating like mad. The performance involved an extraordinary amount of rushing forward to the front of the stage to shout something quickly into a microphone or to shake a maraca and then running off to the back again, gyrating wildly.

The secretaries could hardly hear themselves think, although they didn't seem to want to. Soon they were out on the dance floor under a white awning shuffling their feet to the screaming music. I had thought I might go and sunbathe. I felt a trifle self-conscious taking my clothes off when everyone else was so well dressed, but I had been banished to a tiny section of the pool area, on a couple of blades of grass just behind the stage – for modesty's sake. The security guards – reflector shades, guns – were staring at me emphatically. ('Mayn! Look at those dudes! You think they wanna shoot us down a mango?' Eros had said when he first noticed them.) I was dying to get up and dance and was secretly hoping that someone might come and ask me. I went on a salsa course last summer and Elder Sanchez of Islington's Bar Finca really knows how to inspire a girl. The boys in the band were paying me a high degree of attention but weren't really in a position to ask me to salsa, and in any case I think they were only staring at me because they were wondering why this pale fat women wanted to sit in the direct sunlight at midday.

'Kinda loud, huh?' said a beige-shorted dweeb who had suddenly sprung out of the foliage.

'Mmm,' I smiled above my book.

'What?' he yelled, leaning over my lounger and

dangling his black Ray-Bans in my face from a string that he had round his neck.

'Yes! It's loud!' I shouted.

He pulled up right next to me and had someone bring him a couple of towels to lie on and a bottle of Bud. Keith was his name. Flying planes was his game.

'Well, it's pretty safe, really. Unless you hit sudden clear air turbulence or have, you know, massive engine failure or something,' he said, confused by my suggestion that there might be any danger involved at all.

'And if you do?'

'Then you die. But it doesn't happen that often. It's usually pilot error.'

'Great. Not often, but it does happen, right?'

'Right,' he laughed, writing me off as a psycho and wishing he had sat somewhere else. 'I mean, after I left the air force . . .'

'They kicked you out of the air force! Oh my God. A pilot even the air force wouldn't have!'

'I didn't get kicked out. I quit. And anyway . . .'

I was already mentally slicing juicy bits off his thighs and shoulders to sear over the fire I had made of all the spare copies of *High Life*, or whatever Delta provides, after the plane had gone down over some mountains. Rump steak, medium rare. The pilot never survives in these things.

'So, I'm guessin' you're wishin' there was still Margaret Thatcher to vote for in those elections you're all fixin' to have,' was his next gambit.

'Uh, no,' I replied, peering over the top of my sunglasses and hoping the boys in the band wouldn't be deterred from approaching me by this moron's presence.

'Nope. She totally destroyed the country and initiated a culture of greed and materialism that pervades British society today,' I explained.

'But your economy's doing pretty good, isn't it?' he said, confused.

I don't know why I was feeling so tetchy – I suppose it must have been the sun – but I completely lost control at this stage. I sat bolt upright in my plastic lounger, sweating, red and totally undepilated, and started shouting at this poor man, who was only trying to get laid.

'That's all Americans care about, isn't it? The economy's doing pretty good. The education system and health care might be totally falling apart, basic services reserved only for the rich, ghettos of the underclass on the outskirts of every seemingly prosperous city and all you care about is that the economy's doing pretty good. Well, I'll have you know . . .'

Waiters in white coats glided past us with their trays above their heads, staring. The pool attendants moved away to do their inexplicable sweeping of tiny amounts of quickly evaporating water into grates elsewhere. God knows what was wrong with me, but when I had ranted myself hoarse I eventually stormed off and dived into the water right in front of the band, which was blaring away on one side, and three hundred secretaries, who were sitting sedately over their tapas on the other.

When I went back to get my towel and flip-flops I had calmed down a bit, and Keith was still there, chewing gum and reading Michael Crichton in the shade of one of the speakers. I picked up my stuff, presumably dripping over the most salient passages, and turned away.

'Hey! It was fun talking to you,' Keith shouted. 'You

going to be down in the bar later? 'Bout seven?'

This was a desperate man. The stewardesses must have been put up in another hotel.

'Maybe,' I said. 'I'm off to see the President.'

This was kind of a lie, but it was fun saying it. Dr Alvaro Magaña had once been the President, so it wasn't total rubbish. He was the unwilling head of a short-lived coalition government in the early Eighties, just before things were about to go even more hideously wrong under José Napoléon Duarte of the Christian Democratic Party, Ronald Reagan's puppet who won the 1984 elections.

If you have to live in San Salvador, where Dr Magaña has a house is where you want to be at. The taxi just kept going up and up and up. The potholes began to disappear from the roads and the rubbish started emptying itself from the pavements. Fire hydrants leapt out of nowhere on to the street corners and shops selling designer baby clothes, Italian kitchenware and antiques presented themselves to view. The houses got lower and flatter, less visible from the road, and the people who mill around in town vanished into puffs of smoke. This area was as quiet as a tomb, as manicured as Hampstead Garden Suburb and as rich as The Bishop's Avenue. Only if you look very closely can you see that there are armed security guards hiding behind the hedges, protecting the whitewashed villas and the creeping bougainvillaea.

Marlon, my taxi driver, was happy to have brought me up here. 'Rico, rico,' he kept mumbling to himself, clearly looking forward to his lavish tip. Pathetically, I had left my wallet in the hotel room so I promised to bring his 30 colones out to the Camino Real taxi ranks later. He screeched off down the hill, burning rubber in irritation.

A maid in a blue dress and a white frilly apron opened the front gates and let me into the cool, offering coffee and iced water. The Magañas have coffee-growing interests. She showed me along a sunny corridor and into what was obviously Dr Magaña's study. Although there are thick palms outside the windows and exotic birds squawking hysterically from their branches, the room is like that of an Oxford academic. It is dark and cool in this room, bookcase towering up to the ceiling and leather-bound tomes strewn across the ancient wooden desk. Homer and Ovid, Goethe and Dostoevsky, Dante and Proust. Heaps of paper folders are piled up all over the floor, bursting with tedious-looking documents and scrawled essays.

In fact the only items that mark this out from the average academic's study, apart from the view from the window, are the photographs. And they are pretty striking. There's Magaña and Reagan, shaking hands in a kind of mutual way. It is obvious from the backdrop of flags and the polite distance of the rest of the people the camera has caught the fact that the man who isn't Reagan hasn't rushed forward to shake the President's hand and asked his wife to snap the photo for a keepsake. These boys are on almost equal terms, except that one is the President of a superpower and the other the head of a third world nation with no topsoil and a lot of unruly peasants.

Then there is one of Magaña standing disconcertingly close to Henry Kissinger in a friendly type of way, and another of President Bush looking inordinately pleased to see the guy. I began to feel a bit uneasy. There was a handwritten quote on the wall: *Kennedy – Each time a man stands up for an ideal he sends forth a tiny ripple of hope.* I wondered what kind of ripples Magaña and Kissinger had sent forth between them.

I was interrupted in my cynicisms by Mrs Magaña wandering in to use the well-hidden fax machine. She had wonderfully coiffed and lacquered hair, piled high up on her head in a chestnut sworl. She was in a neat brown dress with a belt round the waist and wore comfortable-looking shoes. 'It's hopeless this thing,' she said, prodding various of its buttons. 'You have to feed each page in separately.' Her English was perfect and she was clutching a sheet of paper with the names and numbers of the different seeds she wanted to order for her garden. Strange that she once had tea with Nancy Reagan.

When I was shown into the living room, my coffee (Turkish) and cold water were on the table and a slight old man was on the sofa. He was smiling and kind with sparkly eyes and energetic movements. 'The doctor told me I should give this up,' he said, pointing at his coffee. 'But I can't.' The trouble, he explained, with being a former president is that they overdo your health care. He said he felt lucky to be getting the medical attention, but every time he had a new freckle on his nose he was being sent off for scans and investigations. 'It's the dentist tomorrow!' he sighed.

The living room had a wall missing and was open on to a little garden, so it was light and buzzing with bright insects. It was also full of orchids. There must have been more than a hundred plant pots of white and purple orchids in the very prime of their bloom. Never having examined them in any great detail before, I can see why they are so closely associated with love. They are the rudest flowers I have ever clapped eyes on in my life and I felt almost awkward sitting there talking to this man about politics and death with these things brushing against my nose. It was impossible to think about anything but sex, and when Magaña told me that he might be able to find out which government troops had been posted to Mejicanos on 17 November 1989 and who the snipers were in the regiment, I was having a lot of trouble keeping my mind off Eros Hoagland.

Really though, my inattention didn't matter, because what the former President really wanted to talk about was England. His children had been at school there and he and his wife were in love with London. He wanted to hear about the new dinosaur exhibition at the Natural History Museum and how much it cost to go round Buckingham Palace. He gave me a book called *Death Foretold* about the Jesuit priests murdered the day before Dad and wrote 'For Anna Blundy – esperando regrese a El Salvador, Cordialemente, Alvaro Magaña.'

It was one of those rare times since I had arrived here that I felt anyone cared about what had happened to Dad or was remotely interested in the issue. Everyone I met was so hardened to violence and so reluctant to feel affected by it that, although helpful, they left me to look after myself. Magaña was genuinely avuncular, concerned that I should find out what I needed to know, and hopeful that I might enjoy myself there despite the circumstances. I wished I had brought some postcards of the royal family with me, or some Earl Grey tea and Bendicks bittermints.

When I felt I had bored him enough, I took my leave of the orchids and was shown into some kind of butch-mobile by his bodyguard, who was deeply unwilling to have a discussion of any kind with me. He reserved the right to remain silent on the question of whether or not he liked paella.

Back at the Camino Real before I set out again I moved rooms and asked them not to put any calls from native Spanish speakers through to me. I wasn't having old KGB Features turning up in the middle of the night if I could possibly help it.

The next day I had a final pilgrimage on my hands.

'I want to see this grassy knoll,' Eros had said as we left. He had asked if he could come with me and Tom, having been on a similar journey himself, out into the country-side to the scene of his father's death. John Hoagland's murder is portrayed in the film *Salvador*, a portrayal which is laughably inaccurate, according to his son. 'It was nothing like that man,' he sniggers. I wondered who had gone with Eros on his pilgrimage and if they had been kind. Perhaps it is impossible to do anything but stay silent in the role of companion. I didn't ask.

We took a taxi and I heard Tom telling the driver why we were going to Mejicanos. He glanced round at me to see the daughter of the dead journalist and nodded to Tom. As we got nearer to Dad's final destination the street became so crowded with the life that had spilled out on to it that it was almost impossible for the driver to negotiate. Suddenly there were little shacks, stalls selling fruit, vegetables, coloured wool, Bic lighters, bright plastic hair slides and bread. People were shouting and fighting and cooking. Children pottered under our wheels. It was, with startling unoriginality, hot and I could imagine how sinister the area would have seemed if there was nobody around at all.

Bill Gentile said it was eerily silent that day and there wasn't a single person on the streets – that's when you knew things were bad. All they could hear was distant gunfire.

We pulled up at the junction between Calle Castro and Calle Poniente, marked by a little sticky '2' on Scotland Yard's barely comprehensible map of the area. This place was a shit-hole. Everybody was desperately poor. There was a church square with a lopsided rusting metal cross in its centre and a few blades of grass in the dust around it. People were lying under the trees, some of them missing a leg or an arm and all of them in rags, rotten-toothed and resigned. Mangy dogs loped about, emaciated and terrified of any human movement near them. A chicken hopped across the road and pigeons flew in and out of buildings sending up grey clouds with every take-off and landing.

The fighting had been really bad here during the offensive and it showed – the few buildings there were completely ravaged and, although there were a lot of people around, they looked as though they didn't belong here, as though they had taken over a deserted place they had never been to before and made the best of it.

Boys called to us from overloaded Toyota pick-up trucks (they seem to be taxis, for hordes of men and women stand precariously in the back of them baking in the sun as they hurtle along at top speed) and women stared.

And there, up on the slope, was the bell tower. 'Your father was paying the taxi and I believe he was shot by the sniper in that bell tower. The guy that shot at me before,' said Tom.

The way the crossroads is laid out, he believes, means that nobody but the sniper in the bell tower would have been high enough to hit Dad where he was standing. Attached to a collapsing church, it is a white, squarish, concrete thing with a rusting bell in its belfry and pigeons perching in its alcoves by the large bullet wounds which mark each long-forgotten murder attempt made on my sniper. Later that day, when Dad was already dead, perhaps one of them was successful.

'Get me out of here,' were the last words my dad said, according to Bill Gentile. 'Arturo [Robles] and I were travelling together that day,' Gentile told me over the phone. He was shocked to hear from me: 'This is a really scary blast from the past.'

'We grabbed your father and dragged him out,' he went on. 'It wasn't clear exactly what happened. We rolled him over and there was a tiny hole in his side. He was conscious in the van.' This was the Spanish TV van that had taken him to the hospital.

In his report to Scotland Yard Gentile wrote that in the van Dad was growing increasingly pale but that there was no profuse bleeding. 'David was a tall man (particularly in relation to most Salvadoreans),' he wrote, echoing what many of his friends had thought at the time – that the fire was aimed above the head of the journalists. 'Dave was too bloody tall,' wrote Bob Geldof in his tribute to Dad, 'and I never saw him duck once.'

1985

It was very late at night at Mum's house and I had been asleep when the phone rang. 'Talk to this man and tell me if you know who it is,' said Dad excitedly. 'No, fuck off,' I said. 'Don't say fuck. Here!' he replied and handed the phone over.

'Hi. I'm Bob. I've just met your father in a bar,' said Bob Geldof, before passing the receiver back to Dad.

'It's Bob Geldof,' I told Dad.

'And is he famous? He says he's in a band.'

'He is famous. He is in a band. It's called the Boomtown Rats.'

Dad was now forced to believe the unlikely-sounding yarn Geldof had spun him. Dad had told him that if his story was true his daughter in England would know because she knew about ridiculous things like pop music, so they had called me to settle the debate.

They became friends and Dad followed Geldof round Africa writing pieces on the way and eventually doing a book, the proceeds of which went to Band Aid. I had a row with Dad about the fact that he was staying in flashy hotels and eating bacon club sandwiches before going out to watch people starve. Didn't he want to take them some food? Didn't he want to donate money? I couldn't understand the lack of compassion. I didn't fully understand the problem.

Geldof picked out presents for me and Dad picked out presents for Geldof's daughter. I have been showing off about this ever since. Can't remember what I got though, apart from a silver cross from Ethiopia.

Ethiopia, 1985: Dear Anna, You will almost certainly never get this card but anyway I sent it. It is very nice here but high – 8000 ft – and hard to breathe. I went over the Canyons in a helicopter. Geldof's left. I haven't. Love Daddykins.

Niger, 1985: Ghastly trip. Millions of mosquitoes. 120

degrees. Sweating horror at night. No food. No water. This could the last postcard. Daddykins.

Niger, 1985: Dear Anna, Here is another card. I feel a bit better now. Niger is nice. Or at least the hotel is. Haven't been out yet. Burkina Faso is awful. Air conditioning – dinners – Gin martini up with twist – Love Daddy

Timbuktu, 1985: Dear Anna, I am posting this from Timbuktu and I'm sure you won't get it. Here's Bob Geldof's signature again.
[Bob Geldof:] We hope to leave your old man here!

Timbuktu, 1985: Here's another card from Timbuktu which I am almost certain won't get to you either. Geldof is wearing a stupid rag on his head. I am too hot to write any more.

Sudan, 1985: Dear Anna, Have just got here. Hot. 106 degrees. Nice view from window of blue and white Niles meeting. Went to have a look round but dark so couldn't see anything. Saw the Mahdi's tomb (you know, the Mahdi) though. Watching tv – the Koran in Arabic, very good. Had roast ant's winkle for dinner. Wish you were here.
    Your beloved father. xx

But wherever my sniper may or may not be now, at 7.15 a.m. on 17 November 1989 he sat up there, squinted into his sights and took aim. I couldn't focus on it. And how is it possible for a person to pick someone off, somebody they don't know, from a distance and kill them? Not to think about their family, their friends, the pain? Quite easily, I expect. Too easily.

Tom was explaining how it would have taken quite a good shot to hit Dad from that position. 'That's why they put him in the bell tower, man,' Eros said. Eros was taking photographs of me. I was taking photographs of the place. I tried to be moved. I tried to imagine Dad falling, the chaos, everyone lying on the ground. One shot apparently followed by a short burst of automatic fire. A sniper and some return fire? I found I could imagine it easily. It had looked safe. No fighting actually going on. It would have seemed horribly calm, but the journalists, used to these situations and protected by their status and their other-worldliness, probably weren't scared. One of them fell. Unlucky. Matius Recart, a photographer, rushed forward with a white flag, shouting 'Press! Press!' It could have been any of them. The government troops were edgy, desperate – the FMLN offensive on San Salvador was going well. I couldn't rustle any sadness up in the straight-forwardness of the situation.

But what did touch me was that Dad was supposedly paying the taxi driver. I could imagine him fumbling in his jeans pockets for scrumpled notes, his glasses falling down his nose (where are they, I wonder? Broken and left there? Retrieved and taken to the hospital? He hit his head as he fell so probably they were broken and abandoned in the panic), his bag slipping off his shoulder, patches of sweat appearing down the back of his shirt from sitting in the hot taxi.

'I guess that would be the spot,' said Tom, aiming a pencil. I guess it would.

★

Afterwards the taxi drove our quiet party home past the Rosales hospital. As we trundled along in the overwhelming heat I felt every bump and pothole as though it was jolting my wounds. This was the first time I had noticed how bad the roads were and how terrible the suspension was in all Salvadorean vehicles. It seemed hotter than ever now as I imagined myself in amazing pain. The hospital was a fucking eternity away. I suppose there wouldn't have been any traffic, so it was probably only about a ten-minute drive, but in pain, heat and a rickety van that is a long way to go.

On our right as we travelled we passed the American polyclinic – a private hospital, brilliantly equipped, efficiently run, air-conditioned and serene. Why didn't they turn in there? Why did they carry on to the notoriously horrendous Rosales – a teaching hospital with barely an aspirin to spare? Who knows. Gentile wouldn't have known about the American medical centre. Perhaps the driver of the van knew a doctor at the Rosales? The three of us sat on the pavement outside the grand colonial-looking Rosales and ate *pupusas*. 'I hate those little suckers,' said Tom, narrowing his eyes in loathing at the sight of Eros and myself having a vaguely nice time. So sickened was he by life in general that he stomped off and left us, running some story about his car being in repair up the flagpole of credibility.

Do you have CNN in your hotel?' Eros asked, pulling his rucksack up on to his shoulder. 'I haven't watched TV in ages.'

We drove back to the Camino Real ('Buenos,'

'Buenos,' 'Buenos,' you have to say to eighteen staff members before so much as getting into the lift) and the maid had shut my curtains to keep in the cool and turned the bed down. The air conditioner buzzed peacefully in the corner. Eros kicked his shoes off and slumped down towards the mini-bar to get himself a bottle of beer. I turned on the TV and found CNN.

'What the fuck has happened to my president?' he giggled, staring at a limping and crutch-hobbling Clinton and flicking the cap deftly off his beer. He tipped back his head and held the bottle up as if he were in an advert for Dos Equis, condensation dripping down his honey-coloured arm and on to his face as the golden liquid slid down his throat.

'Dunno. He was pissed with some golfer and fell over,' I dimly remembered. 'He was in a wheelchair before.'

Eros jumped into the middle of the bed and lay back against the pillows, one arm behind his head. He bounced slightly and beamed at me. 'Nice bed,' he commented, pushing his fingers into the spread. Crisis, dude.

Do I? Don't I? Do I? Don't I? Does he want to? Doesn't he want to? Does he want to? Doesn't he want to? Oh God.

'Yeah. Well. Um. I'll leave you to it. I spend quite enough time watching CNN anyhow. Too much of a good thing and all that. Hope it's informative, but I doubt it. Still, you never know I suppose. Dying for a swim. Hot out there, isn't it? I'll just pop down to the pool. Shouldn't be too many people about at this time, do you think? Well, anyhow, I'll go check. See you in a bit. Help yourself to more beer or whatever, won't you.' He raised an eyebrow at me and I scuttled off in a panic.

When I came back he was watching basketball and he left pretty immediately. He said he'd call me later when he knew what his evening plans were but he didn't. In fact he didn't call the hotel again although he came to the pool one more time. Poor guy almost certainly just wanted to watch the TV, but you never can tell in Latin America.

Chapter Ten

That loss is common would not make
My own less bitter, rather more:
Too common! Never morning wore
To evening, but some heart did break.

And it's not that I pity Dad for the suffering of his death: after all, it was quicker and simpler than some. Nor do I particularly pity myself for the agony of loss any more. I just miss him. Every time I see a little girl holding her dad's hand or riding on his shoulders. Every time I hear certain songs. Eric Clapton's 'Tears in Heaven' ought to be banned on humanitarian grounds. I was on a sunbed in Oxford when I first heard it and I was sobbing so much I had to get off. I was considering suing Clapton for the ten pounds he cost me.

Would you hold my hand if I saw you in Heaven?

You never know when it's going to strike you. I was walking through Notting Hill the other day with my boyfriend. It was very hot and sunny and London smelt like New York. The garbage was rotting and the tarmac was melting and people were cycling about in little vests, roller-skating or driving with their roofs down. Horatio and I were hand in hand, laughing and looking up at the houses we wished we could buy. There were builders with tattoos lazily laying bricks and listening to DJs shouting: 'It is *scorching* out there today! London is *sizzling*!'

Horatio drew his giro out of the post office and I peered down at the pictures of Dodi and Diana blurring the front pages of the tabloids. My beautiful man waved his new money in the air, put his arm round me and said, 'Breakfast!'

Ma's Kitchen on the All Saints Road was empty apart from us, and a huge fan whirred on the ceiling. We linked fingers and giggled at each other and a boy with ginger hair explained to us the (vast) difference between fries and home fries.

'Dodi has unleashed her sexuality . . .' I read, and Horatio scowled at me and my unfathomable idiocy.

Then suddenly this James Taylor song started oozing out of the speakers on the ceiling. 'Winter, spring, summer or faaaaaaall, all you've gotta do is call and I'll be there yeah yeah yeah . . .' My eggs Florentine looked congealy and too brightly coloured and I noticed that the fries were coated in grease. The photographs that earned some photographer millions of dollars in two days were stupid and ugly in their irrelevance, not funny and ironic any more. A blind grief moment.

The first time it happened I was in an Indian restaurant in Oxford. The Taj Mahal. Dad had been dead a few days and I was coping well. I was helping organise the funeral, I was talking to his friends on the phone and I was retaining a degree of dignity. I hadn't realised until then that I was waiting for something. For him to come back, for the pain to go away, for someone to make it all right again.

The curries were finished and the lurid sauces were solidifying in the metal trays. I lit a cigarette and as I blew a stream of blue smoke at my blackened match it struck me that I would wake up tomorrow and he would still be dead. And the next day. And the next. And every day until I was dead too. It was the first time I had taken this in and I sank into the table to cry, knocking a pint glass over and making the dye leak out of the scrumpled red paper napkins.

After that it used to happen every day. Every sad song I ever heard would do it. 'Every time we say goodbye I cry a little . . . the gods above me, who must be in the know, think so little of me, they allow you to go.'

Or, 'Do you gaze at your doorstep and picture me there? Is your heart filled with pain? Shall I come back again? Baby dear, are you lonesome tonight?' Yes.

Now, eight years and some psychoanalysis later, it only gets me every couple of months, and I can usually stop the tears actually spilling over on to my cheeks, but I can still get overwhelmed by this kind of blank grief. I don't feel like talking about it when it happens and I don't expect to get rid of it by crying or drinking or falling into someone's arms. I just sit there until it goes away. I just miss him. I want to see him rapping his fingers on the table, irritably calling a waiter to ask for an ashtray, rifling through the papers and running his fingers through his hair. But I never will.

And it's not exclusive to me, of course.

I saw this tired, familiar and searing pain in the faces of some people I met in Glasgow last year. I was following a mustachioed and gold-braceleted policeman around on his charitable missions, for a piece for *GQ* magazine that never got published. He spoke in cockney rhyming slang and said things like, 'Pass me the dog, me old china.' Dog and bone. Phone.

One of the things we had to do as we hurtled round the country was talk to people in Glasgow who had formed a group called Parents of Murdered Children. It was raining when we arrived and the policeman and his sidekick were quipping away about our supper menu as the taxi dropped us off on a dismal street. ('Chilled melons!? Shouldn't've gottem out on a night like this.' 'Spotted dick!? Ooooh! No thank you.') The grey buildings were black under the sheets of water and we stepped down some iron steps into a basement, holding on to the banister and watching our sodden feet descend before us.

Inside, thirty people were sitting about on those grey, plastic, institutional chairs with metal legs. Doctor's waiting room, school assembly, local council meeting chairs. The room was a blaze of yellow fluorescent strip light and the floor was carpeted in thin grey Brillo pad, polka-dotted with cigarette burns. There were Sunblest, margarine and meat spread sandwiches on paper plates out the back and chicken wings, defrosted and microwaved.

Without exception everyone was smoking. Chain-smoking. Most people lit the next from the last, faces contorted with the effort of inhaling. There was a large china swan with a chipped beak on the mantelpiece over an electric fire. Some of these people, huddled balls of misery, were angry. They stood up while the policeman was talking and screwed their expressions up into loathing and bitterness to shout at him about the shoddy treatment they had received after their child had been killed. But most of them were subdued. They listened vaguely to the promise of things that would come too late for them to care about, and they stared into space, immobilised and desensitised by the screaming pain that had numbed them into torpor and rendered them unable to think about any-thing else, ever. There were pictures of their dead children, cut out of newspapers and Sellotaped to the walls. Some of them had died in sex attacks, others had been murdered by their contemporaries. Most were smil-ing out of their school uniforms at the camera.

It is indisputably worse to lose a child than it is to lose a parent, whom you know from the outset you must one day replace, but that kind of silent despair is the same. I have a very close friend whose twin brother was killed, violently and suddenly, and I see it sometimes sweep over him, provoked by some tiny detail that I entirely missed. His eyes glaze over, he draws on his cigarette more deeply, sighs, looks at his rings, blinks hard and then says something inappropriately flippant and gay.

'So I don't think I'm going to be back for Monday's ses-sion,' I shouted into the receiver, scrumpling up my room service receipt and glancing up at Elsa Klensch ('CNN's Elsa Klensch *is* style').

'OK, no problem,' replied my analyst from his cosy house in Dollis Hill. 'I'll see you on Tuesday at 4.45, then. How has it gone?'

This question completely floored me. How has it gone? Umm. Dunno, really. All right. Bit hot. 'Fine, fine, I sup-pose,' I said. A bit like sitting exams. It's not that it was actually painful or unpleasant or anything. I was just wait-ing for it to be over. Got there. Looked at where he was shot. Went to the hospital. Spoke to some people. Now I want to go home.

I had decided to go for a bacon club sandwich served with chips and gherkins and was just about to pick the phone up when Gene Palumbo called. Gene is a devastatingly kind and concerned man. He asks people questions about their lives as though he cares what the answers are and he asked me to send him photocopies of all the obituaries of my father so that he could get a decent measure of him. I was vicariously flattered by his interest, but I was also pleased for myself – I usually feel so idiotically self-indulgent talking about Dad's murder to people who have probably suffered far more than me. Gene is tanned and open-shirted, but he doesn't look exhausted, bitter and world weary, like most foreign correspondents. He writes for American Christian publications among other things, and perhaps it is his faith that has kept him sane through the atrocities, or perhaps he would be a lovely man with or without God.

'Hey, it's Gene. Listen, I know it's your last night and I wondered if you had organised something, if I could participate. I'd like to.'

Nothing had as yet been run past the San Salvador social directors but I called Tom and asked if he'd like to have dinner. Gene had already been on to him so he had rustled up an adequate pretence at enthusiasm and he came over to the hotel with Gene to get me.

Gene parked his rumbling tank on the main highway outside a shabby, brightly lit café right by four lanes of traffic. Toyota trucks loaded with their cargoes of people hurtled past, frantically chased by buses, lorries and decrepit cars.

There were two plastic tables outside and thin benches at either side of them. We sat down and looked at our paper menu. Basically, the only thing they did for supper was *pupusas*. Tom scowled. The proprietress, whom both

Tom and Gene knew, came out and kissed everyone, said (I think) that she was very pleased to meet me and brought bottles of beer with serviettes wrapped soggily round their necks. She sat down at our table, cheerfully straddling a bench, and played with her long red nails as they all reminisced about the war. From the way she handled her beer bottle and threw her head back to laugh I suspected she was probably another of Tom's heroines from up in the hills.

Gene and I stuffed the pickled vegetables into our cheese tortillas, burnt the roofs of our mouths and watched the traffic rush by in the hot darkness. Tom looked cross.

'There's a transvestite bar downtown that I used to go to,' he said. 'Nobody gives a shit about those people. Nobody. The prostitutes get raped and murdered and it's like not anybody, not your Maria Julia Hernandez or any-one cares. The soldiers used to come in one night and have sex with them and then come in the next night and arrest them all, attack them and shit.' Tom was in a bleak mood.

Gene went home after wishing me a find goodbye and a safe journey, and Tom came back to the hotel. We sat in the bar area with parrots painted on the walls, drinks served from under a straw hut and sad songs piped softly over the speakers. There were lots of tables full of fat American businessmen drinking whisky and talking about investment opportunities. For the first time since I had arrived I wasn't thinking about Dad and was genuinely wondering what drove Tom to live in San Salvador, to do so many dangerous things, to be obsessed with volcanoes. I wondered if he missed his family, if he had ever been married, if he had had serious relationships and what kind of people he came from. He got softer and less angry as he spoke and answered the questions seriously, honestly, swigging from his beer bottle and leaning forwards in his chair.

'And I did have another brother but he died,' he said.

'What happened?' I asked.

His nineteen-year-old brother had been found, when Tom was twenty-one, barefoot, by a roadside, dead, a hundred miles from the place he had been with his friends. No clues. No motives. No suspects. Nothing. Not ever.

When someone tells you something like that, I realised, there is nothing you can say. Nothing comforting, nothing dramatic or shocked enough, nothing to convey the enormity of the sympathy you would like to express. It occurred to me that that is exactly how people feel when I tell them about Dad.

All I could think of to say to Tom was, 'That's some pretty sorry shit, man,' but I didn't. I think I said, 'God, that's terrible', a few times and then ordered some more drinks.

Before he left, at about 1 a.m., I felt we ought to hug or kiss or go to bed or something to seal the intimacy. But we just stood in the bright lobby, pecked each other on both cheeks, shook hands. I thanked him and he went out to his overheated life where he is the gringo in the house by the stadium, and I went back to my neat room, ready to be off to a place where the police come if you call them and people obey parking regulations and campaign for animal rights.

★

When the phone rang at four o'clock in the morning, the dark and stillness behind the curtains was oppressive. HBO Olé was silent and CNN was replaying stories I had watched fourteen times each before going to sleep the night before. None of them seemed to be by anyone I knew – comforting faces that I had seen drunk and laughing, off-air and ugly.

I packed up all my stuff, little things that looked pathetic being crammed into a suitcase – terracotta eggs with miniature wedding or nativity scenes inside them, flags that say *Mi tierra es El Salvador* on them, wooden letters of the alphabet for my sisters to hang on their doors, and a bag of horrible fudge from a stall in the mall across the street.

Tim Coone of the *FT* packed up Dad's stuff all that time ago and checked it out of here for him.

1 dark grey holdall in which is packed
1 leather jacket
1 light jacket
13 pairs socks
1 dictionary
4 key rings
1 pumice stone
1 ½ cartons of cigarettes
1 hotel bedroom key (returned to hotel)
1 return part of air ticket, San Salvador to Miami,
    Miami–Washington.

Etcetera etcetera etcetera. And I couldn't stop myself doing an inventory of all my stuff, imaging which bits would sound poignant on a British Embassy list.

1 packet fudge
1 silver locket

Whatever.

Exhausted, tanned and a bit hungover, I hauled my bags down into the sleepy lobby and drank coffee from a vat, put there specially for people on the early flights out (me). Eduardo on the night shift checked me out wearily, printer whirring, screen bleeping, and said, 'Hope to see you again, Meees Blandy', just as though we were anywhere. New York, London, Paris, Munich.

From the thick blackness a taxi flashed its headlights at me to tell me it was on its way over to the porch. I was beginning to be able to see the outlines of the palm trees, and when the taxi pulled off it was hot air that hit me in the face. The petrol station gunmen were asleep, slumped on their stools in the pinkening light and they looked benign now, drowsy boys on the night shift. Through the clouds of dust on the way out of the city I saw a few people jogging through the dawn. Jogging like Americans jog. They wore Walkmans, white T-shirts and expensive trainers. They looked optimistic, purposeful – as though there might be some reason not to eat and drink yourself into an early heart attack. And there were a few little groups of schoolchildren standing at what were probably bus stops under trees, barefoot, but in recognisable uniforms, rucksacks on their backs, nudging each other and snickering naughtily. Women were lighting the fires at their food stalls and men were setting off somewhere with tools on their backs, smoking and laughing.

The airport was packed and chaotic. 'I'm sorry, Miss Blundy. We don't have your upgrade in the computer,' said Jaime, scowling at his screen, ripping up a boarding card. Not only this but I didn't have a single colon with which to pay the massive airport tax. 'Everybody knows about deees!' It cannot, apparently, be settled with a credit card. I just wanted to go home. I had had two hours' sleep, I was trying to get out of the country in which my father was killed, I had queued for an hour behind three screaming children and I wanted, for the first time in my life, to get on a plane. I burst into tears. They took a credit card.

I was the last person on to the silver machine and I was sweating and crying quite openly by the time I dragged myself up the steps carrying my suitcase, my handbag and my computer. The huge rush of emotion that I had been locking in for reasons of machismo the whole time I was in Salvador, and the relief I felt to have done it and be leaving, the pity I had for Dad who never did leave, all suddenly overwhelmed me.

'Could you help me with this?' I snivelled to a glowering steward, trying to lift my case from floor to ceiling. Please take care when opening overhead lockers since items may have shifted around during our journey and if this thing hits you on the head you will die. 'Sorry, ma'am, we're not allowed to do that,' he sneered, sweeping past me to help someone richer looking carry her bag of crisps. A stewardess smiled apologetically at me from the galley and affected a hobble. 'I'd love to help,' she whined. 'But my I hurt my leg.' I slumped on to the seat-rest and put my head in my hands.

Latin American man to the rescue of blonde woman in tears. He flashed his gold Rolex as he whisked my bag out from in front of me and up into the locker. 'How are you feeling?' he asked. 'Bad,' I mumbled coquettishly and shuffled to my seat at the back of the plane to meet my doom. There was just something about this plane that wasn't going to make it. The woman next to me appeared to have the same feeling and was crying as well.

When the ground and everything you can rely on had conclusively receded and the pilot had decided (in a rather foolhardy way if you ask me) that we could now meander around our spacious coffin, Sourfaced Steward from Hell came to talk to me. 'The gentleman in First Class who assisted you with your bag would like to talk to you and we would be happy to upgrade you at this stage.' I knew baring my midriff would come in handy sometime.

Not only this, but once I had taken my seat across the aisle from my new friend ('Why don't jew come and sit next to me?' 'Oh, well, I thought we could have two seats each. More room!), SSfH produced a bottle of champagne from under a napkin and presented it to me. He followed this by locating two glass flutes and another bottle to open during the flight. My eyes were drying and I was on my way to Miami! I put some moisturiser on.

'Could I have some of your cream?' asked my middle-aged companion, with a leer.

'Certainly,' I chirped, offering him the tube of Vaseline Intensive Care for Hands and Nails.

'I would rather take it off jour hands?' he smirked.

Well, hey, no skin off my nose, so to speak, and I put my paws in his and pulled them quickly away again.

'Do you by any chance know old KGB Eyes with the Jeep Cherokee?' I asked brightly, using his actual name.

'Of course,' answered First Class. 'He is a close friend of mine.'

'I thought he might be.'

Anyway, it transpired that First Class was something big in a Latin American airline. He sounded very pleased about this and showed me a brochure of some kind. What then, I wondered, was he doing flying American Airlines to Miami? He muttered something about arrival times and urgency and looked out of the window. Well, hey, I wouldn't fly it so why should he? Tom Long, in San Salvador, spends most of his life staring into erupting volcanoes. Even he would rather take a two and a half hour American Airlines flight to Miami and get on an American Airlines connecting flight to Honduras than take a half-hour local flight direct. 'I'm not *afraid* of dying, but I don't actually *want* to die,' he explained to me.

On the plane from Miami to Atlanta I sat next to a wonderful South African woman from the same village as Winnie Mandela, who had been married to her husband for twenty-three years. 'I love him,' she said. 'When I look at him I don't see his double chin or his paunch. I can just glance at his arms and I come over all quivery.' She pointed out an ageing businessman over the other side of the plane reading *Newsweek*. We giggled and she told me how you have to learn to enjoy the roar of the engines and the thrust of the take-off. She looked genuinely excited and I did my best. She distracted me by talking about growing illegal drugs.

In Atlanta my flight was delayed because of bombs on the M25 in London. Great. I really didn't want to survive this far and then find myself blasted into oblivion on the M twenty sodding five. I ate little biscuits shaped like fish in the club lounge and made myself gin and tonics. For four hours. But when we finally boarded, I couldn't help being idiotically elated. There were lots of ugly people with sunburnt noses and bad outfits grumbling into their seats and reading the *Daily Mail*. Brits! I was getting a lot happier already. They played us that ethnicky music designed to relax you into ignoring the engine noises, talked to us in Croydon accents and showed us what to do in the event of an emergency. There were Daniel Galvin products in my pink BA wash bag and someone had lobbed me an *Evening Standard* with an appalling racist piece of crap in it about the kind of company Diana was keeping in Pakistan. 'Whatever Abdul Abulbul Ameer she is hanging out with . . .' it read, sickeningly. Home!

I was next to a man with a chip on his shoulder. 'I bet you go to dinner parties, don't you? I bet you've met famous people, haven't you?' he said, judging, apparently, by my hairstyle (lack of = posh) and shoes. 'I have been known to, and, some,' I answered, laughing. Class issues! I really was on my way back and I was fucking delighted.

Eventually Chip and I got on really well and he was telling me that although he had been a Labour voter all his life he was thinking of voting Tory on May the 1st because he felt Blair had sold out. Surreal. We watched *First Wives Club* and raised our eyebrows melodramatically at each other in the good bits.

'Bill was wrong about you,' said a sixteen-year-old to Goldie Hawn, the ageing ex-wife. 'You are *not* Satan.'

When we touched down at Gatwick I hadn't slept for twenty-four hours, I had been drinking fairly solidly for twelve and I couldn't remember ever having been so pleased to be home. London, which always looks so drab and grim when you get off a plane, was sunny and Toytownish. There were shiny black taxis, gleaming red buses, nurses looking *Carry On*-esque in their uniforms, scudding white clouds in an azure sky and children with teddy bears and sweets. It all looked like London in a film from the Victoria-bound train – paper boys shouting out their headlines, cockneys doffing their caps, flower girls with bunches of lavender and men striding across village greens in cricket whites. Most importantly there was a famous newsreader smilingly waiting to take me into his arms and then carry my luggage.

I had been to El Salvador – to Mejicanos, the Rosales, to the Camino Real – and I had come back. Unfinished business completed. A decade of mourning over. I had finally said goodbye to Dad for the very last time. Not only was I still alive, but I felt great. I put my cases down in the middle of my sitting room floor and unpacked my fudge, my little terracotta eggs, my silly flags and the wooden letters for my sisters. There they had been. Here they were.

That evening I went out to dinner with my closest girl-friends, Sophie and Clare, and the newsreader. We walked up the road from my flat in the fading sunlight, past the flower stall, the coffee places, Gap, the Body Shop and Karen Millen. People waved out of their convertible cars to their friends in the pavement cafés. 'Hey! Danny! Where were you last night?!' they shouted above Bryan Adams.

We sat in the rose-coloured glow of an Italian restaurant called Pellicano and ate olive bread, cheese rolled up in slices of prosciutto, tagliatelle carbonara and tiramisu. We drank cold white wine that sparkled in our glasses. I'm not sure I had ever noticed how lucky I was before. I couldn't stop smiling inanely.

I was home.

I had collected a little scrap of each of Tom and of Eros and Gene. I would come back and talk and write about them as though I knew them, just as people talk about Dad. People who have met him in foreign bars, been on treacherous assignments with him, spent a night with him. And all you could ever have of Dad was a scrap, a little splinter of him. I feel as though I spent my whole life clinging to what I could get of him, collecting the pieces he gave me and desperately trying to scrabble back the ones that I felt should be mine – some that he had given to girlfriends, to his work, to his friends. Bits I thought they didn't deserve when I didn't have enough myself. I knew he was slipping through my fingers all the time, like sand through an hourglass, and that one day, when I was least expecting it, it would just run out, slip away and that would be that.

Looking out of my window at that night, just before leaving Salvador, thinking about Tom's poor brother, my poor father, only three hours before my alarm call would wake me, I think it was then I decided I might not try to cling on any more to my desperately escaping father, but that I might just stop struggling and let him go.

There was a particular moment when my life came together, when I suddenly resumed where I had left off that evening of 17 November 1989.

24 May 1997, a month after my return from El Salvador, and my friend Sophie was having a party. I wasn't especially looking forward to it. The Salvador glow was wearing off and, although I was perkier than I'd been for ages, I had reverted to vague detachment – London-

induced stupor. That weekend I had written hysterical lovelorn letters to someone who has not the remotest interest in me, had my trip to Moscow to translate my then boyfriend's televised interview with Gorbachev cancelled and had lost £200 in casinos writing a piece for *The Times* for which I got paid £230. The bloke I had forced to take me Les Ambassadeurs casino in Mayfair had spent the whole time apologising to the croupier that I wasn't losing enough money, saying things like, 'Don't mind us, we're only small fry.'

During the day of the party I had stood around the Victoria Casino in an evening dress having unflattering pictures taken of me by a nice woman who clearly thought I was a dizzy tart. So by the time (6 p.m.) my friend Steve (who had been nominated toastee of the week for his superb three-day extravaganza of grief over a woman he hardly knows) came to take me to Soph's I was in a spitting, scratching evil mood. I had my new black Max Mara dress on, black suede Bruno Magli sling-back high heels and liquid liner. I had curled my hair and felt very *Dynasty* for the time of day.

Humphing, I clacked up the High Street behind Steve to Thresher's and we bought pink champagne because we thought it would be tackiest (the party was called Toasted Again in honour of the hostess's relationship hell and we had been instructed to bring champagne only) and we trundled off to Islington in a taxi. I was only vaguely listening to his story of devastation and heartache. I was more worried about whether or not a certain man would turn up to dance with me later. I suspected he wouldn't. He didn't.

It was still light when we got there and the flat was all

bright, white, pine floors, strawberries, a spiral staircase and hundreds of exploding green bottles. New Labour. New Life. Blair heaven. There were people out on the balcony, framed against the garish sunset by the doors as you approached, waiting for someone with a camera to emerge. I did.

A guy from school that I once accused in my *Times* column of being able to pick pencils up off his desk with his lips told me he was thinking of issuing a writ against *The Times* because it was in fact, if his memory served him correctly, between his upper lip and his nose that he retrieved the items during Russian lessons (Chekhov can do that to a man). Suddenly I felt a hand in the middle of my bare back and I whipped round. 'Sorry. As I did it I suddenly thought perhaps there's another woman with lots of blonde hair who wants to spend all evening talking to Beaky but it didn't seem likely,' he wittered. Giles Coren looked exactly the same as he had when I first met him in 1988, before Dad was killed, before everything went wrong. He was beaming, clean cut and if anything younger looking than he had been then. He swung his champagne about and finished my quote for me when I told Beaky, embarrassingly, that I loved London at the moment 'more than words could wield the matter'.

There was a woman there called Becky with no clothes on and she went out on to the balcony followed by most of the men, whom she would occasionally send down-stairs for another strawberry, much to the ire of their dates. It was a hilarious performance. They all denied fancying her ('too vulgar'), but few of them could drag themselves away from her long enough to say more than that on the issue. She was great —utterly unruffled.

At about 7.30 p.m. I was standing near the door talking to Miranda Green with whom, along with most other people in the room, I had been at Westminster between 1986 and 1988. She was smiling and friendly, holding a strawberry in one hand and her glass in the other. Then suddenly, mid-conversation, something came over me. Or came off of me. Or something. In a flash of I-don't-know-what I came to terms with my bereavement and completely regained the personality (good or bad) I had had when Miranda and I were smoking in the girls' loos at school ten years earlier. I was back. It was a huge and momentous emotional epiphany.

The fact that the party started at 6 p.m. and provided no food and no respite from the lakes of alcohol meant that the whole event was anyway bizarrely and adolescently scandal ridden. By midnight there were couples rowing, people kissing people they shouldn't, announcing decades-old crushes and generally upheaving previously unheavable things. At 11.30 Soph suddenly retired to bed with one of her guests and four feet could be seen protruding from her duvet, conveniently situated in an alcove outside the bathroom. I saw a glamorous, long-haired brunette lean over and kiss a rather unprepossessing young man. 'I don't care how many times you kiss my neck,' he said, a bit churlishly, I felt, 'I'm still going back to Oxford tonight.'

'Maybe I didn't love you . . . Quite as often as I should have . . .' There was no stopping us. Steve is a fantastic jiver. At one stage I half-heartedly attempted to seduce the hostess's brother (who, when Steve had advised me to toast both men A and B and seek out an as yet unlocated C, had offered to take up the role of C himself) but he was too drunk and his ex-girlfriend was making a prior claim. I had not yet pinpointed the object of my desire, but I was certain there must be one here somewhere.

It was at the stage when I was lying on the double bed under the eaves with a glass of champagne and a cigar, explaining why I didn't really smoke or drink to a prostrate, languorous and beautiful bloke who got expelled from school and had a tattoo that I realised (a) that my twenty-third glass ought perhaps to be my last and that (b) this was the best party I had ever been to.

After extremely little prevarication really I left with Expelled Tattoo and wandered off into the night wearing his jacket and looking for the orange glow of a taxi in the champagne blur. What a swell party this was and if we do collide with Mars next July I shan't care because I'm happy, I thought. Or tried to think, but it was getting a bit tricky by that stage.

Although I would have been staggered to acknowledge it at the time, this was the beginning of the first relationship in which I have been able to be unequivocally involved since 1989. The cobwebs cleared and the person I have been looking for for twenty-seven years was standing right in front of me. 'Hey, it's not like I wasn't doing my best to draw attention to myself,' he says, referring to the ludicrous outfits he used to wear in the mid-Eighties when I first came across him. I think I had always been saving Dad's space in case he came back, but now I had finally acknowledged that he wasn't coming back and had been to El Salvador to say goodbye, there was room for someone else.

It feels like coming home. Locks, keys, that kind of thing. I don't feel at all like someone whose father's murder has blighted her life, but more like someone whose father's personality has enhanced it.

Since I remet Horatio Mortimer at that party, this boy I had vaguely known ten years ago at school, everything has seemed so weirdly perfect it lacks verisimilitude. When I went to meet his parents the millstream was babbling ridiculously at the end of the garden, the border collie was lying on the lawn, playfully batted by a kitten, the creator of a gooseberry fool, his aunt, was nursing the scratches she had incurred in her endeavours. A light breeze lifted the corner of the tablecloth. It was just like being in a Helen Dunmore or Iris Murdoch novel. People actually do live like this.

We had arrived in Burford the previous evening, having driven in from London listening to the King turned up very loudly on the stereo of my new car. We picked up his lithe seventeen-year-old sister, Phoebe, at Heathrow and she lay long-legged and brown in the back, holding on to her coiffure and peering glamorously over her shades into the rearview mirror to wonder why very old people listen to Elvis. She had just got back from Sicily and one of the first things she said when she got home was, 'Mum, some Italians might be coming to camp in the field.'

There were chops under the grill and things bubbling on the Aga – potatoes from the garden, stewed fruit from a neighbour and coffee percolating in the espresso pot. I woke up next morning in the 'gold room' to sunlight streaming on to the bed as the shutters were opened on to the croquet lawn and a cup of coffee was positioned by my head. Gold because of the colour of the ancient bedspreads, the glow of the imposing furniture and the light from the garden. There were roses on the mantelpiece. Unreal.

As I surfaced, voices echoed in the hallways and the house was creaking with people going out to church and feeding animals. I got into a deep, iron bath that stood on its own feet and I peered out at the trees. 'Can't we have a row now, or something?' I asked, in the hope that a more familiar scene might arise. Having spent most of the last decade complaining and plunging into the pit of despair, lately I had suddenly become a bit short on subject matter.

We went for a walk instead and the dog, either impressive or pathetic in its grovelling obedience (I couldn't decide which), skipped along country lanes, over stiles, through streams and across dry stone walls with us in the gleaming sunlight. Birdies twittered in their trees, sheep meandered stupidly about the fields and fishes shimmered in the water (except the one we saw a bloke pull out on a hook – that one writhed in agony on the banks – 'Just right for dinner').

At the remote riverside pub we sat on a low stone wall and drank vodka and tonics while the dog gambolled in the water below. Even the bystanders were struck by the uncanny perfection of everything and began frantically to take photographs of the dog and the willows and the fish, in the hope of proving to their friends that there was once a day like this.

More siblings and aunts turned up for lunch in the garden and his brother blared blues out on to the lawn from wide open windows while a string of people carried out bowls of salad, glasses and bottles of wine. Two sisters discussed how their hairstyles had changed over the decades and the under-twenties played cards.

When I got back from El Salvador, everything pulled into focus. I am now present at all these little scenes that I'm sure I probably experienced before, at least in body. But now that I have found Dad again in the mess of the loss of him, I've come back too. When, as a sobbing, pleading, neurotic mess, I told my dear friend Luke Bridgeman about my father he said he thought it was not so much a tragedy that he had died, but a miracle he had lived at all. I didn't believe that then, but I do now. If Dad hadn't died I suppose I would have done better at university, if only to irritate him, and perhaps been able to take work and relationships more seriously. Things might have mattered instead of seeming irrelevant in the face of mortality. And maybe Dad and I would have become adult friends. But now I think I'm just glad to have known him at all.

And the feeling of completion didn't recede. It has got more and more intense. I had woken up from a bad dream. Been let out of prison. Had the storm clouds blown from above my head. Lifted my veil of tears. Any old cliché will do. The nightmare seems to be over.

I had walked straight into and come face to face with the thing I had so erroneously decided had destroyed my life and it wasn't that bad. It was a run-down third world country – quite sad, quite pretty. I could see Dad's death clearly now – as a terrible accident. Not as an awful portent of everlasting despair.

My dad wasn't there. He was here. In my head. In my flat that his life insurance bought. In my little sister's silly smile. In the way the men I like inhale their smoke and tap their fingers. In the fact that I can crack lobster and dive to fetch a silver dollar, and play pool and park a car. In my intolerance and impatience and in my low boredom threshold. In my and my sister's thick hair, sharp eyebrows and wry sense of humour. He was here all the time, waiting for me to notice him and get on with life.

Not without him any more, but with him.

I married Horatio Mortimer on 20 December 1997, seven months after meeting him for the second time in a decade. Out son is due to arrive on 20 June 1998.